A Strong West Wind

A Strong West Wind

A MEMOIR

Gail Caldwell

RANDOM HOUSE

NEW YORK

A Strong West Wind is a work of nonfiction.
Some names and identifying details have been changed.

Published in the United States by Random House, an imprint
of The Random House Publishing Group, a division of
Random House, Inc., New York.

RANDOM HOUSE and colophon are registered trademarks of
Random House, Inc.

LIBRARY OF CONGRESS CATALOGING-IN-PUBLICATION DATA
Caldwell, Gail
A strong west wind: a memoir/Gail Caldwell.—1st ed.
p. cm.
ISBN 1-4000-6248-9
1. Caldwell, Gail.   2. Journalists—United States—Biography.
3. Critics—United States—Biography.   I. Title.
PN4874.C2187A3 2006
070.92—dc22
[B]   2005042682

Printed in the United States of America on acid-free paper

www.atrandom.com

2 4 6 8 9 7 5 3 1

FIRST EDITION

For my mother and sister,

and in memory of my father

1914–2003

So the LORD shifted the wind to a very strong west wind
which took up the locusts and drove them into the Red Sea;
not one locust was left in all the territory of Egypt.

But the LORD hardened Pharaoh's heart, and he
did not let the sons of Israel go.

EXODUS 10:19–20

HOW DO WE BECOME who we are? The question belongs not just to genes or geography or the idea of destiny, but to the entire symphony of culture and its magisterial march—to Proust's madeleines and Citizen Kane's "Rosebud" and anyone's dreams of being someplace, anyplace, else. I was a girl whose father had taken such pride in her all her life, even when it was masked as rage, that he had lit a fire in me that would stay warm forever. I was the daughter of a woman who, on a farm in east Texas in the 1920s, had crept away from her five younger siblings so that she could sit on a hillside and read—a mother whose subterranean wish, long unrevealed, was that I might become who she could not. Each of us has these cloisters where the old discarded dreams are stored, innocuous as toys in the attic. The real beauty of the question—how do we become who we are?—is that by the time we are old enough to ask it, to understand its infinite breadth, it is too late to do much about it. That is not the sorrow of hindsight, but its music: That is what grants us a bearable past.

FOR A LONG TIME, my want for Texas was so veiled in guilt and ambiguity that I couldn't claim it for the sadness it was. I missed the people and the land and the sky—my God I missed the sky—but most of all I missed the sense of placid mystery the place evoked, endemic there as heat is to thunder. You can be gone for years from Texas, I now believe, and still be felled by such memories: Some moment on a silent afternoon—a cast of light, some gesture by a stranger—can fill you with a longing that, by the laws of desire, will always remain unmet.

The truth was that I had been glad to go: that when I drove across the Tennessee River Bridge, I had wept with a kind of wild relief. The morning I left Austin was on a hot Friday in June, and my old Volvo overheated eighty miles north of town; my response was to pull the thermostat, throw four gallons of water in the backseat, and keep going. I drove through remote little east Texas towns named Daingerfield and New Boston, certain that such places divined what I was leaving and what I was going toward. The trunk of the car held an Oriental rug, a beat-up German typewriter, and a quart of Jack Daniel's, and I racked up five hundred miles a day pointed north by northeast, listening to Springsteen and Little Feat. At night, exhausted, I checked in to cheap hotels along the highway, where I collapsed with a glass of bourbon and *Sophie's Choice,* imagining that my new existence would be a female variation on Styron's Stingo—he was a Southern boy, after all; he knew a good tragedy when he saw it; and he had migrated all the way to Brooklyn to become a writer. Irritated by my mother's ordinary concerns, I called her, finally, from New Jersey to announce that I was safe, and that I had crossed four state lines in one day. Because she had spent most of her life landlocked in Amarillo, where you can see halfway to New Mexico without leaving Texas, she didn't believe me—surely even the minuscule states of the East took longer than that to get across. I made it to New York, then Cambridge, days after the summer solstice, that time of innocence and rue when the sun is poised for diminishing returns but seems as though it will hold you in its light forever. It was 1981 and I was thirty years old, and while I scarcely knew it at the time, I had just finished—or rather, launched—an odyssey I'd been plotting my entire life.

I GREW UP in the badlands of the Texas Panhandle, a place so vast and empty that its horizon is interrupted only by grain elevators, oil derricks, and church steeples. This is the Bible Belt, after all, where the daily grain-and-sorghum reports on the radio have to compete for attention with the church billboards along the farm-to-market roads, each of them offering a particular shortcut to heaven. The place was settled by Apaches and Comanches, and later, by preachers, ranchers, and farmers, with the men of

God having the easiest lot: The only crops that do well on the Caprock, besides homegrown salvation, are wheat and grain sorghum. Given the Old Testament weather that defines the country, it's little wonder that religious faith became the cornerstone of the land and the people who stayed. I've seen hailstorms and tornadoes roll in over those fields with no more warning than God allowed Job, and a summer thunderstorm in Texas, which you can smell before it strikes, can be as humbling as it is ferocious. When a blizzard hits the Panhandle, which happens more often than you'd think, the greatest danger is to the cattle—there are no trees or rises of the land to break the wind, and so the cattle can breathe the snow, in its horizontal flight, and drown. People, too, have been brought to their knees for generations by this kind of weather: In the midst of so much nothingness and force, it's difficult not to feel beholden to some larger design.

The skyline in northern Texas was made by the wind, which hammered the place into clay and caliche and near oblivion, then took what was left of the land and carried it farther west. These are truths you don't forget and can't amend; I know now that the angular wheat fields and blank vistas and eerie, lonesome sounds of the Panhandle shaped me as utterly as water informs rock. So mine is a story that begins with the fragments of dreams on the most desolate of plains, where a child came of age listening to the keening of dust storms drown out the strains of Protestant hymns. No plagues or locusts here: just that residing, familiar emptiness, and the ensuing aches and consolations of the journey out.

Is it too much, to feel that the wind carves you in this way? To this day I can hear its howling; I remember, too, being haunted by the stories of pioneer women driven mad by the wind—they simply laid down their brooms, according to legend, and walked out into the vortex, never to be seen again. As a child, I was afraid of the wind as well as the space that allowed for it. The opposite of claustrophobic, I placed my bed in a cramped corner of the room, as far as possible from doors and windows, then burrowed into territories of my own creation. Banned from reading at the dinner table, where I hid books in my lap, I huddled in the closet with a flashlight after bedtime, eschewing sleep for the intoxicating worlds of Mrs. Piggle-Wiggle or Nancy Drew or *The Call of the Wild.* The older I grew, the more elaborate these other realms became. A shy girl in glasses in a do-nothing town, I lived a thrilling life between the pages of fiction; later, prisoner to adolescence, I wrote poems inspired by Ferlinghetti and saturated with melancholy. Year after year I stared at that bleak horizon and waited for rescue. Which, of course, had already arrived. The edifice of print where I continually lost and found my way was my Chartres pointed skyward.

OR MAYBE IT WAS simply my true north. Now here I was, so many miles and years and pages later, having torched most of society's blueprints for a future. I'd walked out on the groves of academe just before they made me respectable, but I was also leaving behind a decade of idealism and excess—and a city whose casualties of history had convinced me not to be one of them. I had been half-wretched my last few years in Austin, hostage to the sort of dark confusion that only youth can manage. I lived on the outskirts of downtown in part of an old Southern mansion, a place with poured-glass windows and eleven-foot ceilings, and I remember waking there on sun-drenched Texas mornings, wondering how it was possible to feel so trapped in a place of so much beauty. I spent my days hurling myself through graduate school and my nights listening to Leonard Cohen's feloniously bleak *Songs of Love and Hate,* or reading *Moby-Dick* in the steadfast amber company of Johnnie Walker. This, too, was a story I had read before, and I knew how it ended wasn't pretty, or even all that dramatic.

And yet somehow fear relented long enough to let me head toward a mirage I had envisioned miles beyond me. The day I drove out of Austin, the only keys I still possessed, besides to the old Volvo, were to a house I had lived in years before that no longer even existed. I took them off the key chain and threw them out the window somewhere near the Arkansas state line, and my breath caught as though life itself had just unfurled. Like a million cowards and trailblazers before me, I had mistaken being gone for being free.

I suppose I thought I was hitching a ride on the narrative that would save me: Surely you had to leave home to write, and to have something to write about, and surely you had to go East.

Besides, I had seen the photographs: a moody and beautiful Carson McCullers at Yaddo; Sylvia Plath, her wide, bright headband belying the torment beneath; Delmore Schwartz, smiling and roguish in a Cambridge yard with snow in his hair. Brazen with hope, I found an attic apartment in a working-class neighborhood, bought a futon and a ficus tree, littered the bare floors with apple crates full of books. Wearing the requisite leather jacket and sunglasses, I walked into Harvard Square, where a tourist stopped me to ask for directions. I took this as a fine sign: Now, I thought with coltish, exhilarated ignorance, now I had bluffed and blustered my way into a wider world. And though it took me a long time to get over leaving Texas—though in some ways I will never get over leaving Texas—the fact is that my heart had clenched in recognition when I got to Quentin Compson's anguished protest at the end of *Absalom, Absalom!* Asked by his adversary why he hates the South, Compson responds with such unequivocal passion that he brands himself forever with his lie. "I dont hate it," he says, and says again, and then to himself, "panting in the cold air, the iron New England dark; *I dont. I dont! I dont hate it! I dont hate it!* "

UNLIKE FAULKNER'S QUENTIN, who loved the promise of death even more than he loved his sister Caddy, there would be for me no bridge in Cambridge to mark my passage out of a brief and tragic life. But I was not the first of my family to leave the

South, and the ones who had preceded me tended to meet with uncertain, even treacherous, fates: aunts who died abroad under mysterious circumstances, uncles who turned their backs on Texas never to return. This legacy—one of half-murmured stories and lonely displacement—had insinuated itself into the family narrative with all the misty persistence of myth, so that the very notion of going far afield carried with it the stamp of courage and betrayal both. My father's oldest brother, Roy, had left the farm in Reilly Springs, Texas, in 1915; the first of ten kids born to struggling farmers, he managed to make it to and through law school at Columbia. He married a Northfield Academy girl, started a practice in Manhattan, became an expert in maritime law. And yet these vast resources—he was a genius, my parents used to say, a *genius*—were not enough to protect him from alcoholism and despair, both of which were in the room when he turned on the gas in a Manhattan kitchen in the spring of 1941. My father, who was twenty-six at the time, went to New York to claim his brother's body. He waited half a century to tell me this story, and when he did, he ended it with a comment that seemed as incongruous as it was grave.

"I saw that dark apartment," he told me, "and I saw the note Roy had left about the debts he still owed. And right then, I swore to myself that I would never be poor."

That he believed poverty had claimed his adored brother, who had helped send him to college, was heartrending to me, but it also became more revealing over time. Poverty and war were the ruthless truths of my parents' generation; if you survived one, it was likely that the other was waiting in the wings. The rest of life's troubles—madness, booze, illness, and premature death—well, these were simply the second-tier calamities that followed hunger and survival. The lives my parents had been born into and struggled to transcend were defined by economic and physical hardship—the bone-weary toil of rural America in the first half of the twentieth century, when the goals were to finish high school, make it to the city a hundred miles away, find the white-collar job that promised headaches instead of backbreaking labor. Roy had scaled these heights easily and then, like Icarus, kept on going.

My father proved his mettle and his loyalty to Roy by staying close to his widow for five decades, until her death at eighty-eight. Helen would marry again and leave New York, but the bond she had with her dead husband's favorite brother never wavered. It was my father's self-appointed duty to care for her in the wake of Roy's death; in their shared devotion, they kept the memory of Roy alive. Though he died a decade before I was born, I grew up with the presumption of his brilliance—and later, when I skidded on the black ice of adolescence, with shadowy warnings about where all that brainpower had gotten him in his last years.

Such sadnesses, for all the obvious reasons, usually blur over time into family secrets, and there is probably nothing more enticing to a child. I cared less about the sweet success stories of my parents' families than the terrible and fascinating ones: the uncle who was struck and killed by lightning in a field, the great-cousin whose tremulous eccentricities had landed her in a state mental hospital (my sister and I called it, with horror, "the insane asylum") down in Midland. Maybe not all children have such gloomy sensibilities as mine. But I suspect that, human consciousness being the cavern of infinity it is, we start off poised for the bad news as well as the good. Even the most innocent imaginations mature under the mantle of child-eating witches and ogres, antagonists who acquaint us with the concept of evil and allow us to bear such a world. For every woeful story I heard mentioned at family gatherings, I had a dozen more that were worse—more shocking and lethal—in the fairy tales and children's books I devoured. Circumstances could change without warning: The pet fawn you raised from infancy could die; you and your family could wind up shipwrecked on an island where a python might eat the donkey. I knew things were going to be tough, and I wanted to be ready.

THIS HARDSCRABBLE EDUCATION had begun with beneficence and grace. My sister, my first young heroine, taught me to read when I was four. A smart tomboy who was two years the elder, she often had to slow down for me; I had a weak leg from the polio I'd had as an infant, and so limped along behind her as best I could. Pam defended me from the less-than-dangerous bullies in the neighborhood—it was the 1950s, after all, and America had barely discovered backyard fences; instead, the clotheslines where housewives hung their sheets became the flaglike demar-

cations of children's valiantly defended territories. I know that,
after taking lip from an oafish girl who continually taunted her
and threatened me, Pam (who must have been all of five at the
time) finally hauled off and hit the child with a toy gun. My father,
delegated to lecture his daughter about the high road of nonviolence, took her aside and gave her a dime.

Such was the world I grew up in: a safe place of renegade
five-year-olds and mammoth-hunting fathers, where sisters accompanied you into the secret forests of literature and dads were
there waiting, back in reality, when harsher measures were
needed. If I could count on Pam to shield me on the streets of
Amarillo, her real patience revealed itself during her first year of
school, when she would walk home every afternoon and
promptly teach me what she'd learned. Alone at home with my
mother, I longed for my sister's return; I am told I would stand
at the curb of our front yard and wait, a young sentinel, until I
spotted her a block away. My memory of this outpost is hazy,
though what remains clear is my arduous encounter, via her
primary reader, with the word *the*. I knew it was important—it
appeared with ominous regularity—but the lack of a hard *t* confused me. Besides, it didn't do anything, this ubiquitous language joint; it had no anchor or tangible correlative. My sister
persevered, as did I, until the word appeared in my mind as the
link it was—a fencepost along the road of text, connecting the
stories that seemed to go on as far as, and even beyond, the north
Texas plains.

No place is a place, wrote the novelist Wallace Stegner, until it takes root in memory and legend. Otherwise, what you have is merely a mountain or a field—Antietam, say, or Little Bighorn, with neither blood nor story spilled upon its soil. With the Panhandle beauty and anomie several decades behind me, my heart contends that the geography where we come of age is defined by emotional coordinates; like Konrad Lorenz's famous goslings, we respond with primal longing to what we first perceive. My landscape of origin had a starkness so extreme that it could signal futility one day and possibility the next, but the evolving narrative that emerged from those Texas wheat fields also had to do with grandfather farmers, with black-sheep uncles who dared to go North, with wayward, unmarried women. My aunt Connie discovered me with her copy of *Lady Chatterley's Lover* when I was eleven, then insisted to my aghast mother that I be allowed to plow ahead—an act of such subversive consequence that I will be forever grateful. Maybe brutish, tender gamekeepers loitered in my future, too; more important, maybe I could find the daring to practice my own brand of abandon.

I must have realized, though, that such bravery or recklessness hardly guaranteed a happy ending. As I grew older, it began to dawn on me that the opposite held true: There lay Peyton Loftis at the opening of Styron's *Lie Down in Darkness,* coming home to her broken father in a casket on a southbound train. There was Wharton's gutsy Lily Bart, who had the nerve and enterprise to maneuver her way into society's loftier realms, only to lie sacrificed on the very cliffs she'd sought to scale. And there, finally, was Roy Houston Caldwell, a man whose story was writ so large that his photograph—a shot of him standing in a snowy field in Texas, his hands thrust into the pockets of his overcoat— still sits on my desk some sixty years after his death. The paths of literature and life alike were strewn with those who had dared to dream or dared to leave. From what I could tell, that kind of gumption promised passion, occasional treachery, and wild, horizontal leaps of adventure. If you weren't careful, it could also kill you.

Part One

Chapter One

POISED AT THE HEART of so much open land, Amarillo, too, sprawled in a sort of languid disregard, as though territorial hegemony might make up for all that loneliness. Route 66 cut through the center of town as a streamlined reminder of what was out there to the west, and the trucks roared through town day and night, slaves to hope and white-line fever, heading for California or just somewhere else. The steak houses and truck stops at either end of the city confirmed these great distances, offering twenty-four-ounce T-bones along with the diesel fuel, and the neon from the all-night signs must have looked from the sky like paths of light—bright flashes of pink and green and white as the town grew sparser, flanked on the highway to the east and west alike by miles of open country.

Downtown in the 1950s was only a few blocks long, and the two banks, the two movie theaters, the Silver Grill Cafeteria, and the Amarillo Grain Exchange were all within shooting distance of one another. The Mary E. Bivins Memorial Library stood on the outskirts of these necessities, on Tenth and Polk, a generous old Georgian mansion with two sets of stone steps up to its wide verandas. The place had been built as a private home at the turn of the century, and its interiors still held traces of domestic calm—

the foyer smelled wonderfully of floor wax and printer's ink and no doubt years' worth of muted librarians' cologne. The books were spread luxuriantly over four floors, with the aisles between shelves feeling as wide as city streets. It was here that an entire generation of kids enjoyed a certain benign neglect in the scorching Texas summers: Scores of mothers deposited their children at the library each day to snatch a few hours of freedom in between the swimming pool and the grocery store. The place was safe, it was cool (in the days before air-conditioning, we had only swamp coolers), and, with its gruff librarians posted like marines between Adult Fiction and the checkout desk, it offered a semblance of day-care-cum-self-improvement. In a city five hundred miles from the Texas Gulf Coast and a day's car ride from the mountains of neighboring New Mexico, the town pools and the library were the closest thing a lot of people had to getting away. Our idea of escape was an order of fries at the snack bar of the Western Riviera—a cross-shaped turquoise swimming pool slapped across the prairie like an SOS sign to God—and then the insouciant promise of the library, where you could lose yourself for hours in sanctioned daydreams.

Maybe such repositories of childhood are always graced by memory, each of them archives of that wider world to come. But for me those rooms were my Elysian fields, possessing a grandeur and reach that would blur over time but scarcely diminish after I had taken flight. My mother drove us to the library in an old Ford station wagon, two-tone Palomino Pink, and I can see it still, idling on the street below, as I half staggered down the stone steps with my weekly haul. There was a limit to the number of books, probably ten or twelve, that children were allowed, and the librarian at first admonished me that my appetites were likely to prove grander than my capabilities. But I was bored beyond measure without a book in my hand, and each week I surprised her by showing up for more.

This doggedness had revealed itself early on, an adaptive trait for a would-be toddler who had struggled to walk until well past the age of two. By the time I finally got to my feet, I stayed there—a victory that must have assured me, on some profound and preverbal level, that determination was a mighty ally. Certainly it proved useful in the library's summer reading contests, where, one sweltering July, our literary progress was tracked by tiny flags ascending a papier-mâché mountain. Each Friday the young explorers would report to base camp to summarize the books we had finished; once the librarian had determined we were telling the truth, she would move our flags closer to the summit. I remember this textual expedition with pain and pleasure both: the giddy journey into higher altitudes, as I left the pack behind, the weekly anticipation of receiving our sentry's seal of approval. And finally, the misery of coming in second to a boy in my age group—I was probably nine—who had dared to outread me.

The realms of athletics and other hand-eye endeavors had found me thus far undistinguished. When she was five, my sister had drawn a horse of such promise that the picture won a local contest; I promptly got out the tracing paper and copied her masterpiece, an act that suggested the visual pursuits be left to her.

5

What I possessed was a capacity to absorb and retain great quantities of words, a skill useful in spelling bees, Latin conjugations, and, for one shining moment, onstage. My dramatic talents were confined mostly to a deep second alto, but I snared the lead in the sixth-grade school play simply because no other child could memorize the lines. Dressed in a red, white, and blue flowing gown that my mother had painstakingly sewn, I was cast as the small embodiment of the American flag. Like a one-girl chorus in a Greek drama, my role was to deliver great swatches of truth and beauty from a pedestal on high. "I am the American flag!" began my soliloquy, then marched on through the ages to the rockets' red glare.

Such fervor must have met with a forgiving crowd in those Cold War and Camelot years. With the native-son exception of Lyndon Baines Johnson in 1964, Amarillo would vote overwhelmingly Republican in every presidential election for the last half of the twentieth century—a conservatism that displayed its colors everywhere from Sunday-morning sermons (where might was always right) to young girls camouflaged as American flags. My father had been a master sergeant in the Eighth Air Force during the Second World War, stationed for three years in a supply-command base in Blackpool, England, until months after the European theater was over. A tall, brown-haired man with pool-dark eyes and a slow, trustworthy grin, he had the type of young-Jimmy-Stewart physical stature that Hollywood had lionized in its soldier-heroes. I was born five years after his return, in 1951, and I grew up cloaked in the sweet mysteries of his having belonged to such an exotic mission. This aura of intrigue was heightened by the stories he told and the ones he wouldn't: the poker games he'd played and won throughout the war, the scar on his chest he refused to explain but that I imagined was a knife wound. Mostly, though, I had a notion of my father as a soldier in charge of a company of men, where his physical strength and bluster-rough camaraderie must have been on full display. For a child, these heroic images were part of a larger dimension that included physical warmth and the smell of coffee and Camel cigarettes; taken together, they offered a portrait of a dad who was already larger than life. When I stood on that stage in my patriotic garb, delivering my lines to a full house, I knew the audience held a man who had come back from the war to take care of me. I must have believed myself at the very center of the home of the brave.

THE WAR NOVELS were housed in the basement of the library, within the larger territory of Adult Fiction, where I wasn't supposed to be. So this was where I headed, preferring the remote aisles of the last rows of the alphabet, where I was less likely to be apprehended. There was a vague warning, issued by mothers and librarians both, to be on the lookout for strange, nonreading men—the ones who smelled of whiskey, nodded off at the reading tables, or seemed too interested in children. I was far too young to consider that most of these dispossessed were veterans of their own wars, real or illusory, and were, like me, simply looking for shelter. They never bothered me and I hardly noticed them, for I was curled up on the lineoleum before the rows of Leon Uris and Herman Wouk—men whom I followed, without anyone's permission, into battlefields and drop zones of untold danger and intrigue.

Did other girls love war novels the way I did, in those years when the national mythos was still dizzy with the aura of Allied victory? I know only that my passion for the genre was probably the beginning of a tragic worldview—that Uris's *Battle Cry* and *Mila 18* would send me on to the grittier likes of James Jones and Norman Mailer; that the moral ambiguities of Wouk's *The Caine Mutiny* may have prepared me for Dostoyevsky in adolescence. If *The Yearling* had been my first literary instruction in grief—in the unalloyed pain of love and separation—then the messy heroics of fallen soldiers only secured that terrible lesson: the idea that valor could face off with evil in a field of mud, and lose.

That's grim fare for a child, no doubt sweetened by the pulpy promise of Uris and Wouk; like most Americans, as William Dean Howells noted, I still preferred my tragedies with happy endings. And not for me the local wars of either Texas or the Deep South. I was bored by literary accounts of the Alamo and the Civil War, though this distinction, in which I eschewed provincial battles for the European fronts of modern war, had more to do with my father than with any sense of regional shame or estrangement. Because he had returned unscathed from "his" war—which had, astonishingly, managed to take place before I existed—I needed to know everything about it. The legacies of World War II were part of the story that mattered most: a home for my unfolding consciousness, with a good-and-evil plot that offered the last vestige of innocence in America.

Our fathers had come home to a nation infused with relief and ideological certainty, two commodities that would never again be in such abundance. Buoyed by the ticker-tape parades and necessary fictions that allowed them to go on, they could look beyond the devastation to a future that promised, at least on the surface, protection from the past. The lines had been so thoroughly drawn by the rise of Nazi Germany and the aggression of Japan that our response was accompanied by a sort of mandatory amnesia—it was essential, if not easy, to overlook the legacies of a Great War two decades earlier, in what was billed as the War to End All Wars. Now we had Kilroy instead of doughboys; now we had the liberation of the camps to justify and amend the casualty lists. And we had Dresden, too, instead of Ypres, but that was a subplot best neglected. If the campaigns in Europe had demonstrated America's valor, the ones embellished by Hollywood and Madison Avenue confirmed it. The darker story, found in classics like *The Best Years of Our Lives* and *The Naked and the Dead,* would outlive the boosterism of the postwar years, eventually becoming part of the elegiac truth about war and modern history. But for now, before the fences went up, we were still a land of suburban war games and toy bombers, where the Nazis always got what was coming and where nobody good ever died—except maybe for a few minutes, only to be resurrected as the other side's troop commander. Our dads were heroes—all of them were heroes, it seemed—and it was our tender burden to be the little soldiers who had made it all worthwhile.

Huddled there in my barracks on the basement floor of the Mary E. Bivins Library, I envisioned myself to be of particularly steely character. Otherwise, how could I bear the horrors of Normandy, or the lousy C rations that awaited me each day? I lived for such extended fantasies, believing that the canned peaches and tinned beef I read about were the food of giants—and that consuming them, in my imaginary way, would nourish me as well. This empathic identification guided me in the real world as often as it transported me into the next. I'd heard all about the fish-and-chips, wrapped in newspaper and sold for a dime, that my father had subsisted on in England; though he described them as dreadful, I ordered them every time I had the chance. Because the grunts in my war novels were, like him, card sharks and betting men, I made him play me at gin rummy or casino until I dropped off to sleep at the kitchen table. It was hardly a parental sacrifice: In the card games and dominoes we both loved, he was already grooming a straight man for his pastimes. He had begun teaching me the bones of arithmetic when I was about four, trying to outfox me by making change for a quarter. I assumed this, too, was part of what made a good soldier: Laugh and shake your head as part of the bluff, never look away from your opponent, and never bet the farm.

No GIRL CAN LIVE FOREVER on blood-soaked heroism and five-card draw, and I still had to train for my relatively peaceful future. I was at the age when compassion and excess go hand in hand,

and I had cried so hard and long over *Gone with the Wind* (not its casualty lists, but Rhett's exit) that my tears had alarmed my mother, then annoyed her. Staggering from Herman Wouk's war stories to the tamer domestic pastures of his *Marjorie Morningstar,* I responded to the exotic constraints of Marjorie's Jewishness by giving up bacon for a month—and, considering my naive day trips into other people's religions, I probably gave it up for Lent. The heroines who seized my heart belonged to the sophisticated urban settings of Wouk's *Youngblood Hawke* and Betty Smith's *A Tree Grows in Brooklyn* or *Joy in the Morning;* if precocious girls elsewhere, poised on the verge of puberty, were reading Austen or the Brontës, I didn't know it and I doubt I would have cared. I was enflamed by the purpler stories that captured the young women of modern America, hoping that, like the field manuals that had given me my father's war, they could teach me how to grasp my life—how to grab hold and ride it to victory.

At a time when television had only a tentative foothold as cultural authority, such moral and practical guidance still belonged to the word, be it secular or scriptural. We learned how to get where we were going by the stories we heard, whether we found them in the classroom, the sanctuary, or the closet with a flashlight. So we listened to tales in the schoolyard about the fates awaiting the craven and depraved, or we plotted our getaways by memorizing the escape routes of Calico Kate or Pioneer Polly. More pious girls, no doubt, absorbed these life lessons from the Good Book itself—"How should we then live?" Ezekiel was taught to ask—and yet the educational merits of Scripture eluded me throughout my childhood. When my parents gave me an inscribed Bible one Christmas, my heart sank with disappointment, then guilt at my ingratitude.

This religious drift was not for lack of access: As the product of a long line of Calvinist preachers and congregants, I had inherited their severity but not their devotion. My mother's hangover from her Southern Baptist upbringing still made her frown upon the idea of cards on Sunday, though none of us, especially my dad, could take her disdain seriously. Instead of the terrifying strictures of a fire-and-brimstone world, my own spiritual domicile held a kind watercolor Jesus with pale blue eyes—a beneficent image I had met in the paintings that adorned the walls of our Sunday-school classroom, where I doodled away the hour and assumed I had a place in His tender flock. My parents had abandoned their strict religious backgrounds when they married, eventually joining a moderate Presbyterian congregation. Each Sunday we were lulled into a nondenominational oblivion by the church's soporific organ music, and it was here, in the light-filled, stained-glass chapel of the Westminister Presbyterian Church, that I discovered something far more commanding than the gist of any sermon. Singing from the hymnal and reading aloud from the liturgical responses, I fell in love with the meter of Protestantism rather than its substance. I took to humming the doxology—"Praise / God / from / whom / all / blessings / flow"—around the house; I startled my mother by reciting, at odd times and without warning, the Apostles' Creed. I was about nine when these epiphanies struck, too young to be considered pious, so she learned to ignore me. "He ascended into heaven," I would solemnly intone, "and sitteth on the right hand of God the Father Almighty, from whence He shall come to judge the quick and the dead."

The quick and the dead! My decoding of this portentous-sounding phrase suggested how I was to feel about Scripture. That God should judge both groups meant, from what I could tell, that the quick were in at least as much hot water as the dead (who, in the soft-hell universe of Presbyterianism, had nothing much to lose). For years I assumed that the quick were impetuous, immoral, or godless; like the "debtors" seeking forgiveness in the King James version of the Lord's Prayer, surely they had done something wrong. When I eventually discovered that *quick* was an archaic term for the living, I was crestfallen. Not only did this new understanding imply that we were all guilty—God judged us every one—but it also meant my interpretation, however wrong, had been more piercing and dramatic than the truth. Far from being chastened by my error, I felt it only supported my prefer-ence for sound over content. I daydreamed my way through a few more years of obligatory religious instruction, the high point of which was my introduction to Catholic services by a friend. The mass at her church was imparted in words incomprehensible in meaning but so rich in tone and cadence that I swooned from the sound. When the time came to select a language in school, I signed up for Latin, then buried myself in its majestic declensions and conjugations for eight more years.

Later, I would learn most of what I knew about other religions from literature—from James Joyce and Flannery O'Connor, who revealed the torment and glory of living under the eaves of Catholicism; from Roth and Malamud, who gave me Jewishness and Judaism with an intimacy I never could have encountered in midcentury small-town Texas. I went after writers who offered mysteries instead of doctrine, who roamed in the wilds of doubt and longing. This seemed to me where God would want to live— out there in the hinterlands, where faith danced and then disappeared. Out there in the war zones, for that matter, where God was surely necessary but sorely missed. All these desires and half assurances awaited me in a world opening more each day, and rarely, if ever, had I been led to them through the doors of the church itself.

So my sanctum sanctorum would remain inside those cloistered library halls, where attendance was optional and devotion absolute—at least for a time, until adolescence offered me darker venues with less predictable results. And oddly, wonderfully, toward the end of that time of single-minded ease, two books I wasn't old enough to comprehend were the ones that had the greatest hold on me. The first was a musty volume called *On the Origin of Species,* and I remember making the childlike association of God and monkeys as I added it to my stack. The librarian looked surprised, then somber, when I handed her the book at the checkout desk, and she waved in my mother from the car. "Gail has chosen something that may be too mature for her," she said softly; unfazed, my mother shrugged and let me take it home. On one level, the librarian was right: I was eleven, and Darwin's findings were way over my head, not likely to keep the attention of a girl who lived for war stories and smaller heartbreaks. But I suspect the woman who declared Darwin off-limits to me, her avid charge, also had more censorious concerns. It was 1962 and we were in the dead center of the Bible Belt; to the east, in Tennessee, Darwin was still banned in the public schools. Before the year was out, America would see the publication of James Baldwin's *Another Country,* Ken Kesey's *One Flew Over the Cuckoo's Nest,* and Doris Lessing's *The Golden Notebook.* Had that librarian any idea what was coming, she might have headed for a fallout shelter and taken me with her.

My other seminal text was a thick, overwrought novel I found around the same time, on an afternoon when I was scanning the recent returns. If by now I was a kid who lived to read, I was still beholden to the action of the page—to plot-driven stories more full-throttle than real life ever was. What I hadn't yet grasped was that prose for its own sake, grown-up prose, could be so transporting as to exist beyond linear narrative in a corridor of its own making. One might call this the beginning of a modernist sensibility; I think, though, that I was simply ready to be a witness to beauty—that my brain was waking up to the world's possibilities, and they came to me by way of fiction. The book I held in my hands that day was a worn hardback copy of Thomas Wolfe's *Look Homeward, Angel,* and I didn't get beyond the first page, because what I saw there so humbled and elated me that I could read no further. "Each of us is all the sums he has not counted," Wolfe had written in his second paragraph. "Subtract us into nakedness and night again, and you shall see begin in Crete four thousand years ago the love that ended yesterday in Texas."

That I had just been given the confluence of time, space, and metaphor—a rough abstract for human consciousness—was clearly way beyond my comprehension. What I knew was that someone, in some other time and place, had made sense of the largeness of life and the dark reaches I felt so privately within my soul, and that this stranger had found out *where I was*—he had said so, right there, with "yesterday in Texas." This seemed to me a secret contract between writer and reader, a grail beyond any promises I had heard about in school or church. I went home and kept the revelation to myself, sensing that I would carry the elixir—great comfort and petition both—through all my days.

PART OF WHAT I was falling for, beyond all that swoony prose, was the author's own apologia for leaving. In the rich and gusty self-portrait that was Eugene Gant, Wolfe had given us one of the early Southern-boy migration stories—a prodigal son escaping the madness of Dixie, catapulted by ego and estrangement toward the distant North. This propulsion, this outward imperative, is part of America's founding story, in history and in myth, and I must have read a dozen versions of it by the time I actually qualified for those shelves in Adult Fiction. A tattered trail of protagonists, most of them alienated and most of them male, would wend their way through my early literary consciousness: Binx Bolling, the perpetual dreamer of Walker Percy's *The Moviegoer;* the young men of Larry McMurtry's early Texas novels, leaving Cheyenne even if they had to crawl; Faulkner's Quentin, who journeyed so thoroughly into my heart over the years that he became *my* Quentin. That so many of these itinerant figures were men did not occur to me; I think I was searching for a flight far-reaching or victorious, however torn asunder the heart that had launched it. The few female protagonists I came across had a tendency to stay put. Should they dare to venture beyond the borders of propriety or domesticity, they often suffered misery, ostracism, or untoward death. I discovered the full spectrum of this punishment for roaming when I got to James's Isabel Archer and other female innocents abroad; for now, as I veered my own boat into the chop of adolescence, I aligned myself with the guys who had hit the road.

Not that Kerouac or his wanderlust forebears had anything on my ancestors. My maternal great-grandfather was a Baptist preacher who had lost an arm fighting in the Battle of Murfreesboro, though this sacrifice is said to have barely slowed him down—one hand, Grandpa Mitchell insisted, was all he needed to hold the Good Book before his congregation. Both sides of my family were Scots-Irish, with English on my father's side and Cherokee on my mother's, and we assumed from our mongrel lineage a sort of moxie, as though we had gotten as far west as we did by our refusal to stop moving. Like a lot of settlers who had migrated west in the mid-nineteenth century, Grandpa Mitchell had pulled up stakes in Tennessee and "gone to Texas"—an explanation, common in the Deep South at the time, that revealed not destination but freewheeling spirit. GONE TO TEXAS was the sign you scrawled and planted outside your house when, like Huck Finn, you were lighting out for the territory, even if you didn't know where you were headed. The resounding theme was one of agency—of staring down your adversary, heading west, trying to outlast whatever trouble awaited you. My mother's father, a farmer with the exquisitely Southern name of Jerome Forest Groves, used to walk the rows of his crops all night long when an early freeze hit Breckenridge, Texas; he believed that his tread on the hard ground would raise the temperature a few degrees. I don't know that he ever saved so much as a head of lettuce. But the notion that he thought he had, or could—well, that was the same endurance that put him on the road during the flu epidemic of 1918, when my mother remembered his walking ten miles into town to get medicine for his children. That was the kind of faith I'd heard about in churches, generally reserved for moving mountains. That was what got you to town, or to Texas, or just got you through the night.

MY FATHER'S FATHER, James Penick Caldwell, known as Pink, made it as far west as Quanah, Texas, on the southeastern edge of the Panhandle, before love took him home to Reilly Springs. Quanah had grown up around the railroad, and Pink went there as a young man in 1890 to find work. "There was a man shot here in town, but not hurt bad," he wrote to the girl he had left behind. "This is a lively little place." Still, Quanah's high life was no match for Della McElroy, who would become my grandmother. A friend tried to convince Pink to press on to Oregon to work the railroads, part of the great westward wave of young men who would build the Northwest. He told Della he was heading home to her instead. "If I was to roam this wide world over," he wrote, "I would not forget my black eyed Darling."

Della wanted to marry Pink, but she was only seventeen, and her father, Dr. J. E. McElroy, thought she was too young. She was physically slight, and because she was stubborn and he knew better than to cross her outright, Dr. McElroy told his daughter she could have his blessing when she weighed a hundred pounds—calculating, as a father and a physician, that she had already reached full size. Della saw the dare for what it was, and she got on her horse and rode it through the creek until her long skirts were drenched to her waist. Then she went home and climbed on the scales, and Dr. McElroy had to keep his word.

I came of age under the rubric of this story, and Della's head-strong guile continues to fill me with gladness: Who was this hundred-pound mass of insubordination who stood up to her father, married Pink, and gave birth to six sons and four daughters? She died in 1936, when she was fifty-nine; my father had left college to go back to the farm and care for her in her last months. I knew her only through the legends she left and through the farm at Reilly Springs, a rambling old white house with no indoor plumbing, each of its rooms bearing whispers of the past. There was the front bedroom where as a boy my father had found a copperhead coiled beneath his pillow, instilling his lifelong fear of snakes. There was the long farm table, occupied for hours each day, where Della had fed her hungry brood in shifts; the ones who showed up late generally got the least to eat. And there was the outhouse—humble, enduring edifice—where a bullying cousin once tried to spy on me and my sister, until my dad got wise to the boy and sent him on a mysterious snipe hunt. Mr. Pink, too, had died before my childhood, just after my father had come home from overseas. But I can still and forever see Della riding through that stream, defying and outwitting her father. It was a splendid lesson for a girl in rough-hewn Texas to possess—my very own *Pride and Prejudice*—and a story my father, in the years that followed, may have regretted passing on with such unabashed pride.

INNOCENCE IS A STATE perceived only after it is gone; and mine now seems a mirror image of the nation itself—or at least of the dominant culture, playing its indolent game of lawn tennis across a darkening sky. In those last years of latency, my pleasures remained pensive or interior: fishing with my dad, climbing trees with my sister to our fort (in actuality, a neighbor's forbidden flat-topped garage roof), where we read and ate pimiento-cheese or butter-and-sugar sandwiches and presumed to defend our secret bivouac. In teaching me casino, a card game based on memory and sums, my father had cultivated what would be a lifelong love of numbers; for years, I feigned interest in his venerated stock pages, both to please him and to prove that I understood fractions. Having mastered these rudiments of math, I dove headlong into the elegance of algebra—a place of labyrinthine and serene precision in an increasingly uncertain world. I remember feeling an easy relief when I got to binomial theorems and x-factors: Algebra's arched perfection was a buttress of clarity for a girl whose showiest asset was her mind. I was short, taciturn, and thoughtful; I ran for class treasurer instead of the deeply coveted post of cheerleader. And if math wasn't exactly cool, knowing how to pass it was. My first education in the casual cruelty of girls came when a reigning cheerleader invited me to her house to spend the night, only to ask me, without flinching, to finish her algebra homework before I left.

Throughout childhood's march, this was the position I would hold—the kid who read too much, talked too little, cried inconsolably over novels even as I maintained a steady grip on my own uneventful life. And then, to my parents' awe and terror, the changes of puberty threw me into adolescence like a bull rider out of a gate. The year I turned fourteen, I grew four inches, got breasts and contact lenses almost in the same week. I started rolling my eyes at the idiocies of Latin Club and Student Council. Outfitted with a supply of Marlboros—they were twenty-five cents a pack—I began hanging out at the local drive-in burger joint, slouched in the shotgun seat of a friend's Mustang and looking for action, listening to teenage wipeouts on the radio. The old 45-rpms my sister and I had worn nearly through, from "Get a Job" to "The Twist," had been replaced by the Beatles, who had stormed *The Ed Sullivan Show* a year earlier; now it was the sleepy, syrupy sounds of the Four Seasons and the Association we heard, about to be rendered impotent by the marvelously dirty lyrics of "Gloria," "Louie Louie," and the Rolling Stones.

What was happening to me, of course, was taking place all over America, but that in itself was a marvel: Radio and TV were creating a mass culture, and my rebellion dovetailed with one of the great cultural upheavals in modern history. Television's response to the Kennedy assassination had proved how a country could be soldered together by the collaborative enterprise of myth and machine: that technology could transform history simply by recording it. The airwaves that delivered rock 'n' roll piped in its language of sedition to every urban alley and backwoods lane from sea to shining sea, and the listeners waiting there responded with the frenzy of a mob outside the Bastille. If Van Morrison's "Brown Eyed Girl" had told us how to *make love in the green grass behind the stadium,* then the Stones' bump-and-grind bass gave us the final permission for those hormonal outrages, and Janis Joplin told us how to scream. For decades, English teachers had been trying to impart the hidden glories of theme and symbol to their unwitting students. Now we were curled up in bed at night with transistor radios to our ears, listening to one of the great antiheroes of popular culture, Wolfman Jack, instruct us in the subversive narrative of rock 'n' roll. Now we were meeting metaphor head-on in the undeniable poetry of John Lennon and Bob Dylan; Paul Revere's hokey descendant, poised to foretell another revolution, had taken acid before his midnight ride. And now, when Country Joe McDonald told us we were all fixin' to die, he made it sound like an anthem instead of a eulogy.

Who could resist such shock waves of grit and grace? I fell headlong into the pop-culture explosion around me, bored senseless with the homogeneity of life before rock 'n' roll. I pierced my ears, illicitly and crookedly, with sewing needles and bottle corks, using ice cubes as my only anesthetic. I wore chalk-white lipstick and nail polish in acolyte imitation of London's Yardley Girl, an early-wave supermodel who was kohl-eyed and anorexic. Amarillo, too, responded to the lion at its gates with radical measures. The Dean of Girls at my high school, a formidable woman known to all as Miss Willie, took to carrying around a ruler to measure our hemlines, and she wielded that weapon as though it were a holy scepter. Once apprehended, we had to drop to our knees on the linoleum floors of the high-school corridors, genuflecting before Miss Willie's mighty gauge. When I was sent home to change, I took the reprimand as a badge of honor; within a few years, I would be wearing far more confrontational garb. Like the rest of the would-be bad kids at Tascosa High, I had to make do with the minor rebellions of smoking in the parking lot and skipping journalism class; the only real trouble we could find involved unlocked liquor cabinets and illegal keg parties.

Except for sex, which in the mid-1960s presented a dangerous territory that many had wandered into but few were willing to acknowledge. As a child, probably in the late 1950s, I had discovered that my mother stashed the best books under her bed, away from her daughters' eyes; this dust-bunny archive was where I found *The Carpetbaggers* and *In Cold Blood* over the next few years. But first there was *Peyton Place,* which I devoured. I was shocked by the idea of Constance MacKenzie's nipples being hard as diamonds, even if I didn't quite understand why they were. Most of my education in sexual desire had come from the elliptical instruction of popular fiction, where women got carried upstairs as a way to end the chapter. So mine were only vague prepubescent fantasies, fostered by novels instead of boys, and then almost accidentally. And that was before I got ahold of Mary McCarthy's *The Group,* which shattered whatever fictions America had left about good girls and chastity when it appeared in 1963. McCarthy had dared to have her women experience sexual bliss and dared to call it what it was; in the American vernacular, the word *climax* would never be the same.

I must have made off with my mother's copy of *The Group* somewhere in the mid-1960s, a few years after it appeared; certainly the fragile paperback I still own, with its background shot of the movie cast, testifies to that. But McCarthy's randy sophistication was more than I could yet tolerate; besides, her characters were Vassar girls, and that was in another country. And McCarthy's novel had, after all, belonged first to my mother. My own self-conscious march into sexually explicit fiction came at around the same time, accompanying another foray into adulthood. I had just gotten my driver's license, which meant I could plant my flag all over the Panhandle, or at least Amarillo, and I remember being surprised and disappointed by what that freedom implied: So what if you could go anywhere at all, if there wasn't anywhere to go? For a fifteen-year-old, such unrestricted vision meant that I could take off in my mother's car for, at most, a couple of hours. But at the time it seemed like a mockery, as though my mobility had opened up the horizon, only to underscore the emptiness of its plains.

Two interior journeys softened this letdown, if only mildly. The first was a novel called *The Arrangement*, by Elia Kazan, a steamy story of a love triangle that I bought one summer at the corner drugstore. The other expedition began when I read a short story in *The Saturday Evening Post*, slightly racy and deep, about the sexual awakening and ultimate downfall of a young woman named Lucy Nelson. It was excerpted from a novel to be published the next year, in 1967, and it had been written by a man named Philip Roth. I had never heard of him, though from what I could tell, a lot of people had. What I knew was that he followed Lucy's chaotic despair toward its natural end; more impressive, he had given his novel the wistful, ironic title of *When She Was Good*. Partly because I was determined not to be, I asked for the book for Christmas. And whether they knew or intuited it, my parents seemed to realize that I had turned a corner with this particular book, and that my path might be veering in a dangerous direction. That, say, the author of *Goodbye, Columbus* might be excavating caverns far more threatening than those of either war or evolution, at least to a teenage girl on the prowl, armed with her Marlboros and her driver's license and her long white nails.

And then I met Travis.

Chapter Two

I HAD HAD OTHER BOYFRIENDS before, most of them as sweet and green as early corn, and nobody of whom my parents would have disapproved. The first had been a boy in seventh grade who had dared to kiss me at the movies after giving me his St. Christopher medallion; I had promptly and mercilessly broken up with him, beginning a long pattern of fleeing whatever was right in front of me. There had followed the usual array of letter jackets and transient dramas; by the time I had survived such tenderfoot follies, I was a long-limbed fifteen-year-old, bored enough to be wild but innocent enough not to know how. One hot spring night I walked into an illicit keg party at someone's apartment, the kind of gathering where teenagers are buoyed by the artifice of cool and the adrenaline mix of glee and fear. And standing across the room, with all the offhanded prowess of a lion surveying the savannah, was a rough-cut, good-looking blond guy, wearing blue boxer shorts and holding a beer in his hand.

Well, how dare he? In Amarillo in the mid-sixties, such behavior seemed either shocking or irresistible, and I found it both, partly because Travis didn't seem to notice or care that he was working the crowd in his underwear. This sort of James Dean charisma defined him, and it explained why I later took to calling him Travis Too Bad in the narrative I told about my life. Travis was tough-guy handsome, and he was sweet beyond measure—at least until he broke your heart, at which time all that charm became as alluring as morphine and as dangerous as an unattended .38.

He was twenty-one when I met him, in 1966, and I was in love with him for an eternity of a couple of years. Though I didn't see him for weeks after that night, it was easy to find out the crash-and-burn stories that surrounded him. Travis had been a high-school football star, which, in the Panhandle, was about two inches shy of walking on water. He'd gone to the university in Austin on a full sports scholarship and become the starting quarterback when he was only a freshman. A college town with a huge student population and liberal tradition, Austin was poised to be the Berkeley of the South by the time Travis got there. And his meteorlike descent was as dramatic and public as his earlier glory. He started taking LSD, went the stories, and didn't care who knew it, then stopped attending classes with the same casual aplomb. True or not, such rumors only added to the luster. Travis lost the scholarship and came home to Amarillo. Now he spent his days in that indecipherably cool activity of boys and their cars, hanging out in an old white '56 Chevy, listening to bootleg Dylan tapes, drinking in the parking lot across the street from Stanley's. Now he was a legend of a different kind, and every parent in town knew it.

He was my first Jake Barnes, I think, my first wounded antihero, felled by hubris or history or some other tragic flaw. Be-

cause Travis had lost part of his ring finger working on a wheat
thresher as a kid, he was classified as 4-F and kept from the raging draft. That made him one of the few legitimate 4-Fs I would
ever know, and the injury had a peculiar distinction—it was not
exactly pantywaist, to be working a combine and sacrifice a digit
to such nonchalant bravery. That, at any rate, was the opinion of
the doe-eyed girl I then was, so much so that I earned the affec-
tionate nickname of "Pup" from Travis's friends, probably because of the way I looked at him. "Pu-u-u-u-p, pup pup pup
pup!" they would call when they saw me at Stanley's, speaking
the universal language one hears from pack males—from mating
wolves, or lions at dusk, or men at rodeos, dispatching the
sounds of love, trouble, domination. I blushed and ducked like
any female pursued by the herd, circled the territory, lit another
Marlboro.

Oh, my poor parents! Because Travis was illegal and knew it,
he sent for me—some younger male emissary called and asked
me out, and a decoy arrived at the door to fetch me, establishing
the pattern we would follow for years. Sometimes late at night,
way after curfew and after Travis had had too much to drink, he
would circle the block in his Chevy, daring on occasion to climb
the fence and come to my bedroom window. Or he would call
the house, giving my mother or father the code name of "Cal
Parker"—an amiable straight-arrow classmate of Travis's, known
for his polite ways with parents. So using the code was my
boyfriend's joke, like Al Capone calling himself Eliot Ness. Lost
to sleep, I would hear the phone ring at midnight—and minutes

later, or at the breakfast table the next morning, my father's quiet, angry rumble: "Who the hell is Cal Parker?"

More important, what had happened to their bookish daughter, known heretofore for what little worry she caused? My parents responded to the horrifying metamorphosis of my adolescence in different and gender-bound ways. My mother, a silent titan under pressure, became grave but loyal; when a town gossip asked her about Travis, she stonewalled the woman and held her head high. My father, more male and less reserved, got his shotgun out of the hall closet. He was the fifth of six boys, my mother was quick to remind me; he knew what the breed was capable of. Besides, this was a man who had spent years protecting his girls, sending their adversaries on snipe hunts or worse, so no Cal Parker was going to present much of a challenge. When the inevitable late-night phone call or drive-by visit came, my father would walk outside—robe, slippers, shotgun—and begin his patrol. Up and down the street he would walk, hup-two-three-four, the master sergeant defending his daughters, clad for bed but ready for bear. Because this was Texas in the mid-1960s, such a sight was less shocking than it was the extreme end of normal. And because my father knew the rules of the game—"Hell, honey," he once told me, "half of life's a bluff, anyway"—he also knew that showing off that gun meant he'd never have to use it. I don't believe the gun was ever loaded on his moonlight mile, and I doubt my father was, either. But the boys who tended to congregate outside my sister's and my windows were terrified of him, and not a little thrilled. Wild Bill Caldwell, they called him, with mollified respect; the name took, and followed him for decades.

Meanwhile I, like Della before me, rode roughshod through my young life in search of some kind of freedom. I was a poker-faced liar, and I invented dates with acceptable boys with effortless sangfroid. On prom night, I pleased my mother by insisting I wear my green velvet formal from the previous year, then threw a pair of jeans out the window to change into once the drop had occurred. I spent the rest of the night drinking beer in an alley with Travis, listening to *Blonde on Blonde*, celebrating my good fortune for having escaped the banalities of crepe paper and the Beach Boys.

With all that craggy, forbidden charm, Travis ruined for me the tamer pastures of boys my age—those little rebellions we're meant to take, those early steps away from family toward the blank slate of adulthood. I had gone straight for the wild man in the crowd (the way Sylvia Plath would describe her first sighting of Ted Hughes, that "big, dark, hunky boy, the only one there huge enough for me"). If we were hardly the starlit or star-crossed poets of the Texas plains, we at least fancied ourselves the auteurs of our own saga—one that belonged to '56 Chevys and back-alley dreams, and that eventually broke all to hell. Travis had moved back to Austin by my senior year, and just as I turned seventeen, when I was about to graduate high school, he married another girl. That he had called first, in the middle of the night, to warn me of this precipitous move hardly took away its sting. I feared I'd been destroyed and my parents were certain I'd been saved, and somewhere, underneath my defiance and my shell-shocked heart, I knew they were right. But I scarcely believed I would live through the cure. Anxious for the liftoff of college that coming autumn, I walked the high-school corridors those last few months with all the self-absorbed wretchedness of a young heroine left at the gallows. As much as I'd wanted to avoid the sentimental trappings of most teenage meltdowns, my own repertoire was starting to sound a lot like the Beach Boys, after all.

"YES, THE TOWN IS DREARY," Carson McCullers wrote about the Southern backwater of her anti-idyll, *The Ballad of the Sad Café,* and that was Amarillo. But for a while, love had made it a dazzling, sophisticated place where everything mattered—a little world infused with intrigue and summer storms, accompanied by Dylan singing "Visions of Johanna." One of the pivotal struggles in the life of every reader, or every introvert, is when the real narrative has to confront, sometimes eclipse, the written or interior one. Waiting there on the brink of my life, wondering if anything, anything, would ever really happen to me, I think I would have torched every story I'd ever read if I'd thought the fire would guarantee a real one of my own. I had read all about what didn't happen to the man in Henry James's satin-smooth nightmare "The Beast in the Jungle," and his fate terrified me. It seemed, too, that it could belong to any of us, were you simply to miss the train, or settle for less, or let fear decide your outcome.

You could surrender the fact of happiness for the fantasy of it, and wind up without either one.

⸺ ⸺ ⸺

WHEN MY FATHER WASN'T WALKING point in front of the house, he was a good-humored, sometimes hilarious man with a work ethic honed by his Calvinist upbringing and fixed by reality. Thanks in part to the help of his brother Roy, he had been one of the few in his family to go to college, and he never let us forget that he had worked as many as three jobs at a time to stay there. He had graduated in 1939 from Texas Tech College, in Lubbock, with a degree in business administration, much of it earned during the Depression years. His education had all but guaranteed him a job at a finance company after the war and an ascent to the struggling middle class—it had taken him out of east Texas and freed him from the hard certainty of physical labor. Vivian, the only one of his four sisters to make it past high school, had gone on to get her master's degree and become a schoolteacher; she and Roy thus assumed, in family lore, the mantle of the Caldwell intellectuals. Vivian, or Aunt Sister, as we called her, had married a physician; when she was widowed in her early fifties, she had returned to the classroom.

These stories formed the backbone of what it took to create your own life—work, willpower, schooling—and my mother's path away from her family's farm in Breckenridge, Texas, had been just as clear-cut. The oldest of six children, she had left home at eighteen and gone to Abilene, seventy-five miles away, where she'd gotten a job as a secretary. It was 1932 and rural Texas was hurting as much as anywhere else in the country, and her mother, my Mamaw Groves, had advised her to go: "Someone's got to get off this place," she told Ruby, "and start earning some money." So she'd been given a compass along with an incentive, and my mother found this direction, this arc toward independence, as liberating as any in her life. She enrolled in night classes at a business college in Abilene so that she could learn shorthand and bookkeeping; when she had mastered both, she went north to Amarillo. She saved enough money to buy her own car, as plucky a gesture of self-determination in 1937 as a young woman might achieve. By the time she met my father, in 1941, she was a knockout twenty-seven-year-old brunette who was indispensable to her boss, and she took orders from no man but the one who signed her paycheck. That was the small-town Texas version of Rosie the Riveter, and my mother wore the role as easily as the dames in those rallying-cry posters wore their kerchiefs and gorgeous biceps.

The lessons here for me and my sister were unstated and unequivocal: that work was a necessary blessing; that education, more than just making you smart, made you free—Ye shall know the truth and the truth shall keep you off the relief lines, untethered to any S.O.B. My father fiercely believed that a woman's ticket to lifelong security was a degree in education—that, no matter what calamity awaited you (a world war, a no-good husband), you could always walk into a classroom and get a job. As conservative as this position would seem within a decade, my father's ideas, his plans for his daughters, were characteristically protective and tough-minded: I don't believe he could bear the idea of either of us being trapped or beholden to anyone for the wrong reasons. In the mid-sixties, even as the country began to vibrate with the first signs of the tremors to come, most girls in white, middle-class Amarillo still had dreams of white, middle-class weddings—rites of passage as pure as they were upwardly mobile, still dependent upon the male for hunting and gathering. Knowing all about those hunters and gatherers and the desultory course their hunt could take, Wild Bill wanted us to be able to get clear of the cave.

"Rise and shine, Sandra Gail! Where are you going to look for a job?" It was seven a.m. on the morning of my fifteenth birthday, and my father was standing at the door grinning, the overhead light glaring through the January dark. That he had brought me a cup of coffee to ease my transition into adulthood didn't much help. Now that I was the legal age to work part-time, this was his insufferable idea of a proper birthday greeting: the coffee, the boot-camp light in the eyes, the can-do predawn drill. Where, indeed? Amarillo didn't have much to offer its untrained labor pool; all I had to offer it, besides my father's enthusiasm, was a bad attitude and the wish to get out. These correlated traits no doubt gave me the impetus to survive a couple of monstrous temporary jobs, the worst of which was taking inventory at Woolco for a few days during Christmas break, a little hell of boredom saved only by my sister's hilarious presence. But my first real job, one in which I earned enough to pay for a semester's worth of college tuition, was a grinding clerical position at the Amarillo Credit Bureau—a terrible and hopeless little place where, unlike Melville's Bartleby, I could never prefer not to.

The credit union may have made a Marxist, or at least a liberal, out of me. Because she loved horses, my sister had finagled a job at the Quarter Horse Association, where she could pretend to be engaged in higher equine pursuits. But I, like Bartleby, served as a mere cog in the wheel of the capitalist machine. For minimum wage, then $1.40 an hour, I typed credit reports (most of them negative) and listened to collection agents browbeat debtors who were late with their payments, usually for new cars or appliances. The agents would phone their list of deadbeats for the day, first coaxing, then bullying, them to pay up. When I was bored, which was often, I would pick up my extension and listen in. It didn't take long to figure out that the majority of defaulters had several things in common: They were down on their luck, easily intimidated, and had Hispanic surnames—if Amarillo had an underclass in the mid-sixties, it was predominantly Mexican American. "Good morning, Mr. Martinez!" Doris, a pitiless collection agent, would trill. "How's that new Frigidaire? Have you found work yet?" A few phone calls later, and Doris would be sending in the repo men to confiscate the Martinez family's washer or refrigerator, no doubt worsening their plight and driving them further into debt.

Faced with the heartless inequities of free enterprise, I dove into the kinder world of fonts. I learned to type fast at the credit

union, ninety words or more a minute, using an old Royal manual like my mother's at home. When I had finished transcribing
my reports, I surreptitiously typed up drafts of the poems I was
writing at night. These tended to be self-consciously bleak and
bad, but they polished my typing skills and let me swirl around in
woozy adjectives for a few minutes before the next debtor's dis-
patch appeared. The hours we kept were from eight to five, with
ten-minute breaks twice a day and a half hour for lunch, and the
time log was unforgiving; at 8:01, a red light on the high wall
clock would switch on over our heads, signaling the cattle call to
get to our desks. Paychecks arrived on Friday afternoons, and
each week, my boss, a tyrannical little man named Watson, would
walk past my desk after my envelope had appeared. "Now, what
are you going to do with all that money?" he would ask, as
though fifty-six dollars before taxes constituted true wealth.
"Save it, sir!" I would reply, cadet fashion, then grit my teeth and
wait for the red light to reappear and release us at five, promising
a weekend free for daydreaming, surreptitious smokes, more bad
poetry.

My professed frugality must have impressed Mr. Watson, at
least enough to get me a decent reference, because after that first
penitential thrust into the world of work, my jobs only improved.
I worked one glorious Texas summer when I was about sixteen at
a grain elevator, a storage facility for wheat and sorghum that
reached halfway to heaven. I was the only female on site and
probably within five miles, and my job was to help weigh the
trucks when they came in—a task that involved little more than

shepherding the men who drove them, making sure their wheels were lined up on the massive scales outside my office window. Because Texas men, particularly the solitary fellows who worked the farms and ranches, were a shy lot, they would shuffle their feet and tip their hats and wait for me to finish. After a few weeks of this—of getting to know me, of sharing a cup of coffee or kidding around—they might venture so far as to ask me out, at least until my boss, a sweet man named Jack Curtis, shooed them away. I slipped out at lunchtime and drove to a nearby drugstore, where I ordered grilled cheese sandwiches with pickles and buried myself in the protofeminist adventures of Ayn Rand's *Atlas Shrugged,* a requisite lunacy for most teenage girls at the time. So the summer was quiet and lovely, just me and the boys and the trucks, and Dagny Taggart with her long legs and blessed railroad.

At the end of the afternoon, when there wasn't much else to do, Mr. Curtis and I would ride to the top of the grain elevator—about a hundred feet high—so we could get a better look at the land and sky. The first day he asked me up there to his piece of the world, the ride in the tiny lift seemed to take forever. At that point in my life, everything was fraught with self-consciousness, and I was anxious about standing so close to this man, who was probably thirty years my senior. The platform of the lift was big enough for only two or three people, and the heights we were scaling lifted the breath out of my chest. But like those farm boys whose trucks I weighed, Mr. Curtis did the right thing: He looked away—the universal code of submission in animals, and, in Texas men, of respect. Then we got to the top, and the lift doors opened out onto nothing but miles of air and light. Standing there in the face of so much space and beauty, I had the split-second insight that everything might be all right—that you could trust people to be kind, that you could outlast your own jumpy nerves, that fear could well give way to winged flight. The land below us looked like the most gorgeous patchwork quilt, perfect squares of amber and gold and green, that any god might ever think to envision, and my witnessing it that day seemed to herald that I was there.

GIVEN MY CAPACITY FOR HOPE, I wonder now why my young life could seem so inconsequential, especially when I was angry. Such is the cruel predicate of biology: the reckless disregard that sends hunters after lions and young men into battle. If we even half perceived in those salad days what perils awaited us, the species would have hunkered down a millennium ago and disappeared back into the molecular muck. Partly protected by all that space, I did my part for danger by driving too fast, attending the standard high-school Everclear parties, and smoking endless cigarettes. On lonesome afternoons I would drive my mother's car out onto the freeway and take it up to ninety miles an hour, going nowhere and aching with ennui. Less physically perilous but just as thoughtless was the way I tossed away my brainpower, or at least concealed and marginalized it. I was bored by the idea of mainstream success and alienated from what the world seemed to offer—one poem I kept from those days dwells heavily on the themes of coffins, societal hypocrisy, and godlessness. And yet I cannot locate the precise source of my anger. For years I thought all teenagers were fueled by a high-octane mix of intensity, urgency, and rage; I know only that what sent me onto the highways, and into my own corridors of gloom, was inexplicable to others and confusing to me. Late one summer night, after drinking rotgut wine with a couple of girlfriends, I stumbled into the sanctuary of the church I was so determined to avoid on Sunday mornings. I sat for a long time in that thick dark, filled with the desolate longings of youth and probably primed for conversion. But no burning bush revealed itself; no voice called from within the whirlwind. Only a half-sense of rest and consolation—the notion that a hard pew in the dead of night was a good place for the weary to go. I went back outside, where my puzzled friends were waiting in the car, and drove them home.

IT WAS AROUND THIS TIME that my father began what I dismally thought of as our Sunday drives. As kids, my sister and I had been bored but tolerant when we had to tag along on his treks; my father's route was aimless, and in the Panhandle, there were few destinations to choose from. But now his itinerary was to chart the path of my dereliction, and that meant getting me alone in the car so that we could "talk": about my descent into wildness, my imminent doom, my mother's high blood pressure.

Thus incarcerated, slouched in the shotgun seat with my arms folded against my chest, I responded to his every effort by either staring out the window or yelling back. I don't remember a word I ever said. What I still feel is the boulder on my heart—the amorphous gray of the world outside the car window, signaling how trapped I felt, by him and by the hopeless unawareness of my years. We usually wound up on the bleak outskirts of Amarillo, and I can see us now against that long horizon, an angry father and his angry daughter, having lost our way. Where once we had adored each other's every move, most of mine in imitation of his, now we were in another kind of dance, wary and fierce. He forgot to tell me that I mattered, to him and in the world; I never would have admitted, to him or to myself, how much I needed him. Our inevitable steps away from each other had become an anguished combat, and there was a world waiting of such fiery possibility that both of us had already been handed our weapons.

My father, far more than I, seemed to sense then that the country was raging, that it was a particularly dangerous time to surrender one's daughters to strange lands. But these things—a war somewhere far away, a civil rights movement over in the Deep South—belonged to the evening news, not to the more intimate treacheries of car rides and deceits and disappointments, and so were rarely addressed on any personal level, not yet. Instead we fought about curfews or bad boyfriends; we fought about straightening up and flying right. We fought about everything but the truth, which was that I would be leaving soon, that I had turned from a girlchild stamp of him into someone just as full of fire as he, but whom he hardly knew—someone who clearly couldn't be trusted not to throw it all away.

I had seen two casualties claimed so far by history, young men who had abandoned their lives and families and the 1-A draft notices they had just received. These men, too, were lighting out for the territory, but their signs, had they dared to post them, would have read GONE TO CANADA. The first was a good friend of Travis's named Marshall, and he disappeared with little warning—I didn't know he was gone until someone from a federal agency came to my high school to ask about him, and Miss Willie (who knew everything, including who knew whom) sent for me. Marshall hadn't given me a clue he was leaving, but I had the immediate and instinctive reaction to send his pursuers in the wrong direction. I told them I thought he might have gone east, to Missouri, to visit his mother, when I knew it was the one place he would never go.

Why I did this—why I chose a path of resistance, without any forethought—was baffling to me in the days that followed, though now my action seems as predetermined as Marshall's passage, which traced the same route as thousands of young men before and after him. I was not yet old or sophisticated enough to understand anything about the war in Vietnam and our increasing involvement there; like most teenagers, I had only the rough beginnings of a moral and political sensibility. But I believed in Marshall—I would believe in him still a couple of years later, when he showed up late one night in Lubbock, bearing only a change of clothes and a copy of *The Picture of Dorian Gray,* when I made him three sandwiches and gave him what money I had before he set out again. By protecting him with my Missouri tale, I was invoking the universal loyalty code that young people have probably relied on since the founding of the nation-state: to trust the members of the tribe and question authority.

My other friend told me he was going. Chuck was a few years older than I, always too edgy and ironic for Amarillo, and we liked each other enormously. As a girl who often wound up the confidante for my sister's boyfriends, I had a penchant for becoming pals with boys, probably because I understood their rough, taciturn affection, and because I was good at hanging out. Chuck had been telling me for months that he thought the war was wrong—in Amarillo, a sentiment considered not just heretical but downright feral. He came by the house one afternoon, as grim as I had ever seen him, and sitting there on the curb, he told me not to worry and not to say anything—that he was leaving, but that he would be all right. A few weeks later, I got word that he had made it to Toronto. I never saw him again.

Such forced mobility put a different spin on my father's dictum to avoid being in the wrong place at the wrong time. It also frightened me, in vague and then inarticulable ways, about just who was in charge—about the dangers posed by the institutions that were supposed to keep you safe. My interior pursuits still belonged to a clearer realm, and reading offered respite from my own fear and wildness—a place where I could learn from nobler archetypes and leave the hard choices to somebody else. But it was difficult in those days to care much about SATs and college boards, or to think that the path in front of me would hold the traditional landscapes of marriage, career, family. The dreams I had were nebulous and volatile, and they involved breaking free of those lonesome, empty plains, whatever it took. In some ways the tempests of my adolescence had set me against myself; I'd found that introspection couldn't buy you love, that poetry helped only momentarily, that straight As and spelling bees were no guarantee of happiness or of knowing where to turn. Worse and more pervasive, I was maturing under the assumption that you should never let men know how smart you were, or how mouthy—a girl's intelligence, brazenly displayed, was seen as impolite, unfeminine, and even threatening. So I twisted and turned and kept quiet; when I dated a boy who liked George Wallace, I rolled my eyes and looked out the window. And the smarter you were, the more subversive you had to be. If this attitude was never voiced in my family, it was taken for granted within the cultural atmosphere of the mid-1960s. Girls could excel in traditional fields— English, say, or languages—so long as they didn't flaunt it, or pretend to be superior to males. But God forbid they should try to carve a life out of such achievements. God forbid they display a pitcher's arm, or an affinity for chemistry, or analytic prowess in an argument with a man.

My revisionism in kind was unconscious but thorough. I neglected anymore to mention the mysterious test, taken at age seven, that had resulted in my skipping second grade. By the end of high school, I was lying to my peers about my scores on placement exams, and I blew admission, with private relief, into the National Honor Society. The summer before I left for college, in 1968, I had to declare a major; I took a deep breath and wrote "mathematics" on my admission forms. And when friends asked me what I'd chosen, I lied about that, too.

⋅ ⋅ ⋅ ⋅

THE LAST JOB I HAD IN AMARILLO, at the local newspaper, was the one that mattered most, not because it made me an ink-stained wretch (though it may have contributed), but because it showed me a work world where eccentrics reigned. Like a lot of city papers at the time, the *Amarillo Globe News* was a twice-a-day paper, morning and afternoon editions, and I worked in the morgue, which is what newspaper libraries used to be called. Every summer the *Globe*'s book editor, a tiny woman named Mary Kate, would hire several high-school girls, usually ones who had been good in English, to help her clip and cross-reference both editions for the archives. The tools for this trade were a T square (for ripping the articles), several red wax pencils, and the formidable organizational skills of Mary Kate, who could tear and annotate an entire edition by midmorning. The rest of the day she spent rummaging through advance galleys, reading, or writing her reviews, which tended toward the idiosyncratic in both selection and opinion. We were her starlings, busy and loud, and we hovered around her, filing clips and drinking coffee, pretending we were part of the news business. The glamour of daily journalism revealed itself in the characters who lorded it over us in the newsroom: the society editor (a soon-to-be-obsolete concept in the trade), whose inch-long red fingernails held a constant cigarette; the sports editor, whose aversion to deodorant ensured our aversion to him and his surroundings. On slow days we got to deliver the mail, which meant an hour spent roaming the back corridors from the composing room to the presses, where the smell of printer's ink—from then on eliciting the memory of dirt, work, and happiness—competed with the scent of the lunch shop's homemade roast beef.

Was there anything sweeter than this easy innocence, where a girl discovered the mazes and customary pleasures of work that mattered enough to get her beyond her own brooding self? I loved the newspaper: the camaraderie, the roast-beef-and-mustard sandwiches, the uncomplicated fact of spreading the truth to the world with ink and paper. Had I any doubt of the grave importance of this calling, all I had to do was look up Travis's name in the archives when I got bored. There he was, cross-referenced under "football, high school," winning touchdown after touchdown until his flame went out. And there I was, suspended in the insular bubble of youth and geography and nursing my little tragedy, waiting for the wider world to explain to me what tragedy really was.

The instruction came on a morning in early June, in 1968, two days after Bobby Kennedy had been shot in Los Angeles and a day after his death. Part of our job at the morgue was to archive the news and wire photos that hadn't run, usually because they were redundant or imperfect. In rare instances, like this one, the unpublished photos were far too raw—too ghastly and distressing—to have made it into the paper. I stood there holding the manila folder I'd picked up to file—"Kennedy, Robert F., assassination of," Mary Kate had written—and staring at close-ups of a fatal gunshot wound to the head. It was my first encounter with the intimacy of death, with the idea that it could be sacred and profane at once, and so my glimpsing it that day, in that accidental way, seemed both a privilege and a shame. I had been twelve when JFK was killed, and I'd watched with the rest of the world as the public mythology of his assassination unfurled on television. Now I was seeing his kid brother in a parallel agony, the unedited version, in photos that no one was supposed to be able to bear.

The images were transfixing and horrible, and I knew, on some leaden, primitive level, that what I was looking at revealed something about the greater world—the real world—that I hadn't been able to grasp until now. Here was Camelot's disaster, Abel's execution, Raskolnikov's evil, careless gesture. Here was the grim illustration, without sound track or voice-over, of all those tragedies and war stories I knew by heart.

These are the lessons that history omits: the changing of the guard, the news photos that don't run, the sensibility emerging on an empty plain, like Shakespeare in the desert, shaped as much by absence as by knowledge. The next several years of my life would be a montage of such fractured realities, personal suffering exposed or overexposed, enlarged by history or a wide-angle lens. But for me, frozen before this black-and-white icon of private and collective sorrow, the moment was a collision of fact and understanding. I knew that the secret these photos held was precious and awful. That this was what death really looked like, and how the story could end.

Chapter Three

ABOUT 120 MILES SOUTH OF AMARILLO, Lubbock, Texas, is a prideful cow town with a state university and a prairie dog colony almost as big as its student body; historically, the prairie dogs have been more raucous than the students. The city has spawned a number of musical legends, among them Buddy Holly, Joe Ely, and Jimmie Dale Gilmore, and so Lubbock holds an exalted position in C&W lore. Because it lies in the center of the huge, blank mesa called the Llano Estacado, at the southern end of the High Plains, the town is prone to severe weather—to hailstorms, dust storms, tornadoes, an ever-present wind. Coronado named the Llano Estacado in the sixteenth century, and it didn't change much for the next three hundred years, until farmers and ranchers founded Lubbock and then the Santa Fe Railroad came south and gave it cause to stay. It's a place so desolate and flat you can see the mesquite trees bending from the wind over in the next county, and you can hear a mockingbird from a mile away.

When I went there in the fall of 1968, as a freshman at Texas Tech, I hung a SKI LUBBOCK poster on the wall of my dorm room—a wheat-colored, monochromatic print with nothing but a black horizontal line across its center. I learned to love Hank Williams, Sr., in Lubbock, listening to his crooning heartaches at the corner drugstore near campus, where I drank endless cups of coffee and played "Cold, Cold Heart" and "Honkytonk Blues" on the in-booth jukebox. Lubbock was where I broke a wrist dancing the Cotton-Eyed Joe, learned to wear jeans so long they scraped the ground, went to my first rodeo, my first protest march, spent my first and so far only night in jail. I met girls who were champion barrel-racers and who hailed from small Texas towns named Plainview and Floyd and Comanche, the last being notorious for the sign it had posted during Reconstruction warning black people to stay away; a century later, the advice was still being heeded. I spent two years in Lubbock, wonderful, dreadful years, and by the time I left I had replaced the SKI LUBBOCK poster with a grainy close-up of Bob Dylan and a picture of Joan Baez and her sisters, smiling under the antidraft legend GIRLS SAY YES TO BOYS WHO SAY NO.

First, though, Lubbock was where I learned the pleasures and perils of autonomy—the unsentimental education in self-actualization that college, or leaving home, is supposed to be. Thrust into a five-hour honors course in calculus my first semester, when I was seventeen, I floundered, then panicked—I was one of four females in a class of thirty, and the male professor, when I sought his counsel, told me to drop the course; my board scores made less impression than my gender. Now I am appalled by his wrongheaded advice, though not by my decision to heed it. Calculus frightened me. Where algebra and its older siblings, trig and geometry, offered clarity and precision, calculus was elegant but enigmatic, full of scripts and imponderables and fourth dimensions. It took away all the safety nets and promises that my early exposure to math had offered. If I wanted that kind of ambiguity, I could go back to novels—to Dostoyevsky or Faulkner, where it seemed the real mysteries lay.

And yet my academic wanderings in the next few years had far less to do with math or literature than with the wider world and its increasingly urgent life-and-death allure. Who cared about zoology or Plato's analogy of the cave, when body bags were the endless ellipses of the evening news? Once I had fled mathematics, I declared seven majors in as many semesters, none of them rivaling the competing events of history on the streets. I had started college the same year as the Tet Offensive, the My Lai massacre, the King and Kennedy assassinations. When LBJ appeared on television to announce that he would not seek reelection, he had the face of a man who had aged two decades in four years. In France, the Sorbonne had been shut down by student uprisings against the war in Vietnam, and nine million workers, to show their support, went on strike.

In Lubbock, I shadow-danced to these seismic shifts, happening beyond our isolated wheat fields but not outside the vicinity of our awareness. The cowboys who took me to C&W dance halls or rodeos gave way to guys wearing shades or driving motorcycles; Joe Cocker was starting to sound a whole lot cooler than George Jones. The tough streak and surly alienation I had faked, then cultivated, throughout high school now found an edifice large enough to house all that and more, in a youth culture that seemed ready to torch anything more enduring than Jerry

Rubin's last idea. Life past Amarillo's city limits had gotten me over Travis with the shocking alacrity of youth, and now I found myself a boyfriend—this one was eight years older than I—who had a 750 Yamaha and hair longer than mine. I ditched the cowboy boots for a poncho and suede-fringed moccasins. I writhed to the maniacal moans of Led Zeppelin, mourned with the rest of stoned America over the surreal, backward-lyrics fantasy on "Strawberry Fields" that Paul was dead. We'd traded down *Walden* for Woodstock Nation, tragedy for the melodrama of *Easy Rider.* The long arc of history seemed remote and irrelevant, and we jettisoned intellectual cornerstones as capriciously as we shed bourgeois fashion. I started reading Camus, or pretending to, and shopping at Goodwill Industries. And now, when I went home to see my father, I was wearing battle fatigues of my own.

Like my peers and every youth generation before us, I was mostly innocence and hunger bumping into hormones; what set us apart, what elevated ordinary rebellion onto history's stage, was the bloody backdrop of a theater in Southeast Asia. Literature had long ago taught me that the truth was a messy business, full of half measures and misapprehensions, and the iconography of my culture confirmed it. Rock 'n' roll insisted that we could no longer believe the man in charge; poets and writers had been saying as much for centuries, but now their message had an incendiary cast—if you read *Howl* or *Tyrannus Nix?* when you were slip-sliding through adolescence, Ginsberg and Ferlinghetti sounded more like ambulance sirens than the elegiac riffs of their predecessors. *Time* magazine had shocked the country in 1966 by placing "Is God Dead?" on its cover; the editorial query still lives in memory because a lot of people feared it was true. You could look in almost any direction, toward battle-strewn landscapes from Mississippi to Berkeley, and see that the story line had changed. If we had any omniscient narrator at all, it was Walter Cronkite.

TWO WINDSTORMS—an arrest and a tornado—marked the end of my tenure at Texas Tech and sent me farther south to Austin. In the spring of 1970, when the region's few trees and many prairie dogs were emerging resplendent, the Lubbock police broke down the door of my boyfriend's house at four a.m. and arrested us for possession of marijuana. They had gone to a nearby friend's house first, and because not much happened in Lubbock, their forays made the front page of the local paper, under the headline FIVE ARRESTED IN PRE-DAWN RAIDS. We had been awakened by the sound of men running outside the house. The police found a negligible amount of grass, a couple of pipes, and a lot of psychedelic posters, all of which must have seemed as menacing as uranium; once we got to the city jail, we were treated like dangerous celebrities. I shared a cell with a woman who had been picked up for soliciting. For breakfast, the jailer brought us fried bologna sandwiches, black coffee from a bucket, and a cigarette apiece.

Someone, not I, called my parents, who made the two-hour

drive from Amarillo to spring me. When I saw them standing on the other side of the bars, their fury contained within the grim set of their faces, my heart stretched violently against itself: I loved them, I wanted them to go away; I hated them, I couldn't bear that I had hurt them. My father wouldn't speak to me and could hardly look my way, though he had immediately arranged a personal recognizance bond for my release. They bought me a cheeseburger, then drove me to the home of one of Lubbock's most established criminal lawyers, where I sat feigning sullen nonchalance. Because the belief was common that marijuana began the long, hellish path to heroin, the lawyer checked my arms for needle tracks. He cautioned me to stay away from unsavory characters, by which he meant anyone who had ever smoked a joint or gone to an antiwar demonstration, and told my parents he would do what he could.

Three days later, during nationwide protests against Nixon's invasion of Cambodia, four students were shot and killed by the National Guard at Kent State University in Ohio. The camera canonized the Kent State slayings with the photograph of a devastated young woman kneeling over her slain classmate, but for those protesting on other campuses, the deaths were personal and complicated, and they stripped away a glaze of invulnerability we had taken for granted. The college antiwar movement was a privileged and protected enclave—we were largely white and middle or upper class, we had student deferments, nearly half of us were female. Khe Sanh was a nightmare, but only by empathic consideration; those were not our bodies being unloaded from military transports on the evening news, and they were not often our brothers' bodies, either. If students against the war had yet to grasp the class and race delineations of the Vietnam draft, Kent State blurred the boundaries, at least symbolically, and placed the troops and the protesters on the same side of the barricades.

Hundreds of thousands of people across the country responded to the Kent State killings with mass demonstrations. More than five hundred colleges and universities were closed; at the hotbed University of Texas at Austin, the streets held ten thousand protesters. In Lubbock, a few hundred miles to the northwest, the turnout was tamer. About three hundred people showed up at our candlelight vigil, which drew almost as many counterdemonstrators, many of them cowboys, who had arrived armed with rocks and rotten eggs. Two men with cameras who turned out to be plainclothes FBI agents were there, too, for what seemed the sole purpose of following me around—me, with my high-flown attitude and my junk jewelry, certainly as much a threat to national security or Lubbock peace of mind as an angry nightingale would be to a weather pattern.

I went to the Kent State vigil not out of defiance, but from raw outrage: How could I abide by the words of some lawyer my parents had hired, particularly when it came to matters of conscience? Besides, the horror of Kent State—of kids being gunned down by other kids in uniform—had lessened the sting of my potentially felonious circumstances. I might have a criminal record now, but at least I still had a life, and I wasn't going to waste a minute of it employing restraint instead of passion.

In the mathematics of memory and experience, we know that our perception of time's passage is correlative to biological age: Time blurs into sleepy uniformity when we are children, then accelerates alarmingly as we age—as the length of the present diminishes in relation to the past. Yet there is nothing quite like the brilliant languor of those days on the cusp of adulthood, when the moments are etched with so much color and meaning and hope. The more lurid histories of the 1960s and '70s have gone after the tabloid drama of the casualties suffered instead of the quieter legacy of lasting change. But for a serious girl with too much space and time on her hands, the sheer force of those years gave me a cause as well as a catapult: I was able to see that a life meant something, that you could throw yourself past whatever fate awaited. That you could outlast your father or resist him altogether, even if it broke his heart and made him mute with rage.

Decades later, my sister elaborated on my father's anger during those summer months of 1970. "It wasn't that he was mad at you for trying drugs," she told me. "He was mad at you for getting caught." I took great comfort in this wry assessment, coming as it did years after the resolution of our long battle, where my father's outrage met consistently with my frozen resistance. My sister's version corroborated the man I knew and loved, the one who had taught me how to hunt and count, who believed me smart enough to do anything I chose, including steering clear of small-town police.

They had no case against me, Bill's wrong-place-at-wrong-time warning having been my only real offense. The charges were dropped a few months after I'd returned for the summer to Amarillo, where I worked a dismal job, faked church attendance, and listened to Chicago and the Moody Blues in my room until my mother threatened to smash the stereo. Still, she was happy enough to have me there at all. A week after Kent State, days before I would leave Lubbock for good, a mile-wide tornado had torn through the center of town, killing twenty-six people and injuring more than a thousand. Tornadoes are capable of capricious ruin: They can raze a house to splinters and leave a flowerbed or a child's truck untouched next door. When the Lubbock tornado hit, my boyfriend and I were in a calm spot of town two blocks away from his apartment, and by the time we got home, an uprooted tree was splayed across what had been his living room.

Like the rest of movie-made America, I'd been audience to the film version of transcendent wind tunnels, storms that could whirl you away to magical kingdoms and then bring you home again. The real story, the Texas story, was less redemptive. My grandparents' farm in central Texas had a storm cellar about twenty yards from the house in case we had to run for it; bunkers in tornado country were always placed far enough away from the main buildings to protect you from flying debris. I remembered being four or five and crouching with my mother in the bathtub one night, when my sister and father were away and the sky had turned the death-silent green that always signaled a tornado. So I knew the truth about such things—knew that real tornadoes, however spookily beautiful, promised not visionary insight but potential disaster, and that all you could do, besides head for a safe zone and cover your head, was pray. That, like so much about the weather and the nature of the Panhandle, it didn't help to put up much of a fight.

THE DRUG ARREST gave my parents whatever ethical consideration they thought they needed to search my room, so random checks were conducted at will and without apology. But I had little more to hide than the skin I was shedding, most of the transformation recorded in the purple-haze prose of a summer journal. This metamorphosis, though, was probably more frightening than any arrest, since neither of my parents, with their arsenal of rage and reserve, could do much to inhibit its progress. That spring I had discovered the radical-psychology movement, and I was carting around R. D. Laing's *The Politics of Experience* as though it held the secrets of a new Revelation. One night my father, on arbitrary patrol, appeared in my doorway with the Laing paperback in his hand, his eyes dark with confusion and what I now know was pain. "What in the hell has happened to you?" he asked me. "Have you lost your mind?" And I wanted to yell *Yes, of course I have, this is what Laing is all about: "If I could drive you out of your wretched mind, if I could tell you I would let you know."* So there stood my father, gruff and handsome and now the enemy, probably as frightened of me as I was of him, and I wish now that I could have been kinder, or exempt from the cruel long divisions of youth. But no answer I gave him would have made things right, or even much more bearable. The world for which I yearned was burning, and nothing—no amount of either shelter or lockdown—was going to keep me from the beauty of those flames.

Chapter Four

HOWEVER MUCH THE NOTION might have horrified my
preacher ancestors, Austin was to be my city on a hill: the little
utopia where I believed my best self might emerge. When John
Winthrop invoked the Sermon on the Mount in 1630—"We shall
be as a city upon a hill"—he was speaking as much to human
capability as to heavenly vision. In Austin, where the renowned
Texas sunsets oversaw dreams and delusions with nonchalant
parity, it was easy to lose oneself in a sort of holy madness; all of
us, in those days, were acolytes to some higher cause. A stronghold of old progressive politics bumping into hedonism, the city
had long invited such enthusiasms. Any day past three p.m.,
sometimes sooner, you could find a surplus of half-drunken leftist lawyers at Scholz's Beer Garden, plotting the revolution and
trying to pick up women. A billboard on Nineteenth Street, later
renamed Martin Luther King Boulevard, announced the division
between the haves and have-nots to every incoming student at
UT; because the undergraduate population was nearly forty
thousand, the message politicized a lot of kids. WELCOME TO EAST
AUSTIN, the sign read. YOU ARE NOW LEAVING THE AMERICAN
DREAM. BE AWARE OF RATS, ROACHES AND PEOPLE WITH THE LACK OF
FOOD, CLOTHING, JOBS AND THE AMERICAN DREAM. When Eddie

Wilson and Jim Franklin, a rock entrepreneur and an underground comix czar, got the idea for Armadillo World Headquarters—a beer garden that went on to house much of Austin's rock 'n' roll fame—dozens of carpenters, electricians, artists, and ne'er-do-wells showed up and worked for free until the place was finished. Austin had Barton Springs; it had the legendarily progressive *Texas Observer;* it had the infamous One Knite, a bar so seedily hip that even the feds liked to brag they'd hung out there. Most of all, for a decade or two, it had a community of creative rogues and prophets who saw each day as a rough cut for celestial bliss.

This idyllic notion wasn't hurt by the fact that the city was poised in the middle of Texas lake country, a profusion of waterfalls and rivers that widened in an indolent sprawl toward the Gulf of Mexico. The place was so beautiful, and so fey, that the fantastic threatened to eclipse reality all the time. Busloads of hippies were known to make pilgrimages to a granite marvel west of Austin called Enchanted Rock; if the geological formation didn't glow and sing of its own accord, as legend dictated, the hallucinogens ingested on the way would ensure the show. One of the first food cooperatives of the era began when a couple of guys with a truckload of oranges rented an empty storefront, christened it the Twenty-ninth Street Food Co-op, hauled in the oranges, and opened the door. During the dedication ceremonies of the LBJ Library, in the spring of 1971, the antiwar demonstrators outside included a group of women dressed as witches who put a hex on the building. Six of them were arrested. A year later, a crack appeared in the structure that no one, not even the engineers, could explain.

That kind of power is not without its price, and the cost of Austin's terrible beauty could be high. If the city was a nexus for bohemian lifestyles and radical politics, it was also a place where a lot of people lived hard, scary lives at near-warp speed, and some of them wiped out altogether. The narrative unfolding around us was so perilously intense that it was easy to forget mortal dictates, or the cautionary laws of gravity. Tear gas or a night in jail seemed like a negligible sacrifice when men our age or younger were losing a leg or a mind, walking point some ten thousand miles away. We believed—we knew—that our job was to re-create the moral center: Our supposed role models and leaders had gotten us thus far to Hue, to Nixon's White House, to Watts and Selma. Such convictions produced miracles as well as lunacy, and you couldn't always differentiate between the two; we were living in an era when Diane di Prima's so-called poetry counseled stocking up on codeine, come the revolution. It was like standing in a high wind every day, and stepping in almost any direction meant free fall. This promise, or danger, made a lot of cliff-walkers believe they could fly, or at least take the dive and walk away. We were stardust, we were insane with hope, we would live forever, if only we could keep from being killed.

My first exposure to Austin's subterranean enclaves had been in the late sixties, when Travis took me to the Vulcan Gas Company, a place that championed the likes of Muddy Waters and the Velvet Underground before most of the world had heard of them.

Now I was in the city unleashed and beholden to no one, youth's apprehension having fast given way to euphoria. I signed up for Latin and philosophy classes, befriended a young Quaker woman from Louisiana who knew every antiwar group in town, and joined the Student Mobilization Committee in time for the huge fall protest marches to the state capitol. I wandered, barefoot, across the campus green, wearing the peasant blouse and torn blue jeans I would live in for years, pretending to read Herbert Marcuse and Norman O. Brown, two alleged architects of the sexual revolution whose results seemed far more scintillating than their prose. I had found a boyfriend just back from the Sorbonne who murmured to me in French during our brief attachment, and who believed it his duty to educate me in the existentialists. He gave me a translation of Jean-Paul Sartre's *Nausea*, and though I can no longer remember my self-appointed tutor's name, I still have the book. And I have kept the piercing memory of sitting on the university mall one afternoon, within view of the Main Library, with its massive inscription in stone from the Gospel of John: YE SHALL KNOW THE TRUTH AND THE TRUTH SHALL MAKE YOU FREE. I was immersed in *Nausea*, falling through space with its effete narrator as he realizes the limits of his own remove. Later, Roquentin's miserable discourse would hold less sway. But at the time I ached with the description of a character's self being so violably transparent, so much so that his own consciousness had made him, for a moment, "the root of the chestnut tree" at which he gazed. This was Walt Whitman's worst nightmare—it was Sartre, singing the body static. I had little idea of who Sartre was or whether he mattered. I knew only that I was stunned with the vastness of the imagination, the provinces available if you were brave enough to go there, and then I looked up and saw the quote from John 8, and I started to cry. I cried for how blessed and frightened I felt, poised at the beginning of the path, faintly sensing all the lights and shadows that awaited me. I cried, I think, for the innocence I knew was behind me—shed in that Lubbock jail, or maybe grieved for in my father's eyes, but clearly absent from the fundamental bleakness, which I had recognized, at the core of Sartre's thought.

One of the highlands of learning in anyone's life is that time when one recognizes both the heights and limits of self—that epistemological thundercrack when the entire landscape and one's position on it are revealed. Calculus, or perhaps merely the calculus professor, had shown me the first insurmountable boulder in my path. With my young would-be existentialist coach, I was beginning to glimpse a pattern that would hold true for years: The men I knew, many of them exceptional, had a tendency to either corral or discourage me. They wanted to teach me about jazz or dialectical materialism, even if I cared for neither; they brought me their little gods—their methodologies and their deconstructionists—and laid them like voles before my feet. But I was rarely compliant enough to reap either the rewards or the penalties of true devotion. Casting about for a calling that first year in Austin, hoping to understand the infrastructure of revolution, I enrolled in a course in Marxist philosophy, which turned out to be so mind-numbing that I went to sleep in class. I took careful notes during lectures on writers from Kafka to Wharton, writing in the margins, just as carefully, "I disagree." And though I finally settled on English as a major, I had a near-physical aversion to the way novels were eviscerated in class; when the inevitable discussion questions came—"What is Flaubert trying to tell us?" "What does his use of images convey?"—I felt squeamish, even embarrassed, without knowing precisely why. The party line on the classics usually eluded or annoyed me. Emma Bovary was supposedly loved and loathed in equal measure, but I didn't know how anyone could feel disdain for the woman, whose emptiness seemed to me a wounded consequence of the world in which she lived. Tolstoy's purported moral condemnation of his fallen heroine in *Anna Karenina* escaped me altogether; caught up as I was in Anna's catastrophic spinout, I assumed he adored her as much as I did. Somewhere deep beyond reason, I believed in characters as their creators' golems—they were spiritual beings, it seemed to me, molded from clay and given life, who could then do whatever they pleased. However idealized this projection, it may have helped me challenge my own superiors. When a professor refused to hear my rebuttal after we disagreed over Guy de Maupassant, I walked out on her class.

Such indignations were not always earned; would that I had been as compelling, or even as rebellious, as I imagined I was and hoped to be. I was merely young and slightly feral, and no great mentor had yet staked a claim to my heart. A maverick attitude may have saved me in the long run, safeguarding whatever originality I possessed. But for then it simply set me free, in the most anarchic sense, and sent me bounding into the wider world, propelled by a joyous disregard for any semblance of authority.

All of which made me like a million other kids pretending to be adults at the time, and half of them, it seemed, were in Berkeley or San Francisco. My newfound sense of independence was soldered to my mobility, in defiant contrast to having been landlocked in the Panhandle all those years; surrounded by seas of wheat and sky, I could scarcely believe I would ever get out. Now I saw that the opposite held true: All those places I'd visited in books were accessible realities, had I the courage and volition to go looking—to trade in my role as spectator for the drama itself. I had quaked when I read Tolstoy's description of Ivan Ilyich, facing the past from his deathbed, as a man whose life had been "most ordinary and therefore most terrible." This verdict seemed an inevitability of bourgeois culture; true or not, the assumption was in keeping with a lot of what I saw around me, and it was frightening enough to be pivotal. A year before I was to graduate, in the summer of 1971, I was enrolled in an intensive Shakespeare course that met daily and was mandatory for my degree. One Friday morning after class, I told the professor that I wouldn't be there for a couple of weeks—that I was heading for San Francisco and would be back to class when I could. He half sputtered his surprise, probably more at my blithe attitude than anything, then told me attendance wasn't optional and that I would have to choose. So it was to be *Othello* or Berkeley, and I didn't even blink. The next week I hitchhiked the 1,800 miles to northern

California with a couple of friends, on a route that took us through Amarillo in the predawn hours and out I-40 heading west. The last ride we got was in an old black panel truck, bearing a bumper sticker that you often saw on the roads in those days: YOUR DAUGHTER MAY BE IN THIS VAN. We drove all night, and by dawn we had made it all the way to Berkeley. Someone shook me awake and I looked out the back window onto a pastoral, tree-lined street, where I saw a banner for People's Park hanging from a balcony and a Viet Cong flag in a nearby front yard. This did not seem to me the setting for either a terrible or an ordinary life.

The next few weeks began a wanderlust courtship with northern California, and with cross-country travel, that would last a decade. I hung around Telegraph Avenue, where underage flotsam and young radicals with painted faces and ferocious plans pretended they knew what they were doing. I slept on somebody's kitchen floor, walked into a bar on a Berkeley street corner and found Jerry Garcia jamming in the back room. The San Francisco Mime Troupe was skewering Nixon in performances at Golden Gate Park; harbor seals were mating on the rocks at Point Reyes, on the way to Big Sur and Mendocino. I had never imagined such casual magic, where the days seemed to repay you with incandescence just for walking out into them.

When I got back to Austin, I dropped the Shakespeare course, already abandoned in theory, with no second thoughts. And then years later, when I was reading *King Lear* on my own, my heart filled with remorse over what I had lost—or rather, what I feared I had lost, since the terrain of regret is always illusory.

How could I have turned my back on the grail of English literature, on so much lasting depth and beauty, in exchange for a few weeks of flash and dazzle? And yet the path I chose now seems as preordained as those routes of my ancestors. Ambivalence would be the central tension of my life over the next few years, the compass gone wild as it swung between the tame direction of the social order and the thrills of my frontiers. Several months after the Berkeley pilgrimage, beleaguered by the detachment of academe, I dropped out of college—an act I perceived as one of stunning liberation. It was the spring of 1972, eight weeks before what would have been my graduation, and the gardenias and azaleas were in bloom all over Austin.

I THINK NOW OF KAZUO ISHIGURO's tragically circumspect butler in *The Remains of the Day,* his life so devastatingly compromised because he could not bear to look at it head-on, and sometimes this seems to me the central predicament of the introspective soul: Do we contemplate the life, or fling ourselves willynilly into its path? Do we measure out its passions with coffee spoons, as Prufrock laments, or do we stop musing altogether and go after the pulse of consequence? Decades later, I know only enough to feel the chill of the dilemma—sitting in this wintry domain with my dog and tea and so much silence.

Chapter Five

FREE FOOD TODAY! The spray paint was Laurel's idea, but someone else had thought of the target, a grocery store notorious for its crummy labor practices. The artistry took place in the middle of the night, and so by dawn, the entire front wall of the building, facing an Austin thoroughfare, was emblazoned with Laurel's two-feet-high guerrilla script. By evening, she had been arrested and released, and the story was on its way to becoming legend. Every revolution had its strategists and jesters, and Laurel's little insurrection appealed to both. The message in FREE FOOD TODAY! had all the elements of good street theater: Its satire was eloquently precise, it fingered the capitalist rapscallions, and it was a deadpan illustration of democratizing the narrative.

Austin in those days had the casual habit of setting itself on fire. Laurel's action was typical in an era when graduating seniors could be recast and reclassified as outside agitators the minute they left college, when the utopian community we envisioned was being invented as we went along. Reification was the great structuralist argot at the time, and we were reifying all over Austin: Autonomy was a farm collective, liberation a wall mural or an all-girl rock 'n' roll band. By the early 1970s, the city was a model of hip institutions: progressive law offices, free counseling centers, restaurant and food co-ops, newspapers and printing collectives. If you needed a meal, you went to Sattva's, the pinko-vegetarian restaurant in the Methodist Community Center, where for a couple of dollars you could get Squash-the-State casserole, beans and rice, and a plateful of salad—no iceberg lettuce, though: The farm workers were on strike. If you needed Lukács or Emma Goldman or Carlos Castaneda, you went over to Grok Books on Seventeenth Street, where I sometimes worked the cash register. If you wanted a hash pipe, you walked around the corner to Oat Willie's, and if that pastime went south, you could find a people's lawyer in one direction and a drug-counseling center named after Tolkien in the other. Part of the radical beehive within the old University Y building, across from campus on the main drag, Middle Earth was open all night and staffed with people who were kind, savvy, and accustomed to crisis. The stairwell and foyer were covered with arcane mystical notices, Che Guevara and STRIKE! posters, and upcoming-ride boards for hitchhikers; so many weird establishments had been at the Y over the past decade they could have levitated the building. Middle Earth's warren eventually made room for Womenspace, one of the first feminist peer-counseling centers in the country, and this transition testified to the motley aura of the zeitgeist. In the mid-seventies, when women's self-defense classes were on the rise, you might see stoners, feminists, and kung fu enthusiasts passing on the stairs; it was often difficult to tell whether the yells coming from behind closed doors were war whoops or bad-trip distress cries. There was a grand, if at times fictitious, feeling of cama-raderie to all this: We were outlaws and underdogs, as Dylan had said, people who believed that our firebrand version of love and anarchy would ensure a new cosmic righteousness, or at least end a war. It was like a sitcom shot in black light, except that all of it mattered and all of it offered a half-dozen reasons to get up the next morning, because the world was there, languid and dazzling and filled with mayhem, and waiting for you to change it.

My leap from academic familiarity into the rough country of my new life was eased by all these institutions, half of which I worked for or loitered at, sometimes both, over the next few years. I got a job running the office for a blackguard attorney who taught me a lot about criminal procedure; with equal determination, Brooks instructed me in the arts of consuming Scotch and steak tartare, customs he considered critical to the practice of law. He was a legend in good-old-boy circles for his ability to shoot from the hip and win. Because he was usually too hungover to get there on his own, one of my expected duties was to drive him the two blocks to the courthouse. He'd swallow two tranquilizers on the way, then bolt from the car with his legal pad, blank except for the name and docket number of his defendant. A couple of hours later he would reappear at the office, eyes gleaming, his temporarily freed defendant in tow. In court, he displayed what the boys in the courthouse hall would have called *cajónes:* He would leap to his feet, mumbling and protesting prosecutorial folly, hollering (often without reason), "Motion to set aside, Your Honor!" and anything else he could think of to interrupt the proceedings and get the judge's attention. Brooks was a good lawyer. But this was Texas in the LBJ years, when the miasma of cronyism that permeated politics extended as well to the halls of justice. There were plenty of stories about the whiskey links between lawyers and judges (one judicial luminary, having put away half a quart of Wild Turkey, fell out of a deer blind one afternoon and broke his leg), and a lot of ex parte business was conducted down at the Oyster Bar or Scholz's Beer Garden. Brooks belonged to the force field that included judges and politicians and half the hellraisers and misfits in Austin, several of whom were writers, and whom, along with the raw steak and Scotch, he considered part of my education: Gary Cartwright and Bud Shrake (the title of Shrake's novel, *Strange Peaches,* had entered the Texas lexicon as a phrase for the absurd), and especially Billy Lee Brammer. Billy Lee had written one of the great political novels of the modern era in *The Gay Place,* and he had never recovered from his greatness. He was up and down in those days, crashing from speed and from the good run he'd had, and he spent a lot of time in Brooks's front office talking to me, probably because he knew it would keep him out of trouble for the day. He turned out not to be as strong as his worst impulses or the methamphetamine that stopped his heart a few years later. Billy Lee died in 1978, when he was forty-eight; I was twenty years younger, and had only just begun to understand how fine a book he'd written and how rough and sad the life had been.

I FED AND WATERED BROOKS'S GUYS as though they were cattle, with a little care and duty both, and they responded with a loyalty, poignant to me now, that was equal parts Texas chivalry and the docility that is often wildness's underbelly. They found me houses to rent and bought me a steak every so often, and if they tried halfheartedly to date me, the hippie girl some two decades their junior, it was only within the comic bounds of a sort of big-brother flattery. When a notorious loafer-architect in the gang had too much to drink at Scholz's one afternoon and reached for one of my breasts, I poured a beer over his head, to the uproarious approval of the rest of the table. Most of them knew where the line was in the sand, and after that, they wouldn't cross it.

My fondness for Brooks and his gallery of thieves and dreamers was a serendipitous footnote; it was his profession that had brought me to his door. My father had wanted me to go to law school, a dream no doubt derived from his brother Roy, whose legal career in New York had been phenomenal before his death. With the resistance that by now defined us, I announced I would become a paralegal instead, devoting my untrained talents to saving the downtrodden and the criminal masses. The rebellion was safe but piercing: I had picked what my father most desired, then waved its black-sheep alternative in his face.

Privately, though, beyond its edgy glamour or potential for social justice, I loved the law for its magnificent span. Its corridors of reason were the one place I had glimpsed where intelligence and ethics seemed great enough to protect humanity from itself. I worked at a series of law offices in the next few years, places where *progressive* and *radical* were as crucial to the résumé or shingle as a higher degree, but my devotion was ephemeral. One spring afternoon, feigning boredom but more lost than I knew, I took the trial law-school entrance exams with a stopwatch on the table and a beer in my hand—a determinedly nonchalant position that only masked my fear and confusion. The stopwatch would show I could conquer law school if I chose; the beer was a surly insistence that I didn't have to try.

Beyond and in spite of me, beyond all the dropped courses and conscious misfires and throwaway career plans, a certain private education was already under way. Taking a cue from all those fictional characters I had left behind, I was shaping my own golem: my image of fertility and liberation that would lead me through these thickets to some broader shore. If I had turned my back on institutions of higher learning, I still kept to my heart the words I had found there—the components of a moral life that can't be teased apart until the mold has taken. When a friend, intent upon political self-education, asked me for a reading list, she supposed I would send her to Marx or Marcuse; instead I told her to start with George Bernard Shaw's *Man and Superman.* What I had long suspected to be true about women—their private sadnesses and silent, well-stocked prisons—I was finding revealed without mercy in novels from *The Portrait of a Lady* to *The Bell Jar.* My understanding of race and racism came from the primary sources of *Invisible Man* and *Native Son,* from black writers whose words wrenched and enlightened me in ways no ideologue had ever come near. I read Langston Hughes's "Let America Be America Again," and I heard there the same rhapsodic petition that drove the oratory of Martin Luther King, Jr. If Hughes had shaken my heart, he had also awakened in me the shame of a white girl's insular naïveté, about what I had either ignored or misunderstood.

The part of Texas I grew up in was so white it hurt your eyes; the Panhandle's minority demographic may have been primarily Hispanic for geographic and economic reasons, but the fact remained that black people didn't choose to go where few black people had gone before (remember the town of Comanche). At the end of a civil rights movement we had experienced mainly on the evening news, my high school class—a student body of six hundred—had a handful of black students. One of them was a willowy, handsome track star, and we made a stab at liberal sophistication by naming him class favorite. (This well-intentioned gesture was undercut by the fact that nobody had bothered to get to know him before the election.) Now thrust into a college town where antiwar activists were often in collusion with black community organizers, I was getting a crash course in the infrastructure of human error and iniquity. I read Thorstein Veblen and Michael Harrington and C. Wright Mills, then Lillian Smith's *Killers of the Dream,* a white woman's memoir written in the 1940s, and I felt exposed and heartbroken by her first sentence: "Even its children knew that the South was in trouble." I learned that the war I loathed in Southeast Asia was being fought by a disproportionately large number of black Americans, young men who generally lacked the social and economic wherewithal their white counterparts could use to avoid the draft. Race was a four-letter word, I was beginning to realize, a labyrinth so large and intricate that even the likes of Faulkner and Malcolm X combined couldn't fully apprehend it.

I either didn't see or didn't care that, in shunning academe but holding on to the canon, I had walked away from the house but kept the bricks used to build it. My lineage was full of such rogue dispositions, born from necessity as well as enterprise. The frontier preachers of my family were just Bible-reading men who had stepped up to their holy obligation on an empty plain. Granddad Groves learned to work as an oil pumper because he had to; my father, a superior poker player during his years in England, had later used these talents—nerve and numbers—to master the stock market in his spare time. That I was electing to ignore the blueprint for a life but keep the draftsman's tools would have surprised no one in my family, had they been able to see beyond the immediate and unsettling picture of my renegade path.

Which was ever-widening, roaming as I did between the streets and lairs of Austin and points south and west. Freed from what I perceived as the upwardly mobile demands of post-Puritan society, I did what I could to pay the bills; the job was especially appealing if it didn't require my actually showing up. When I worked at Grok Books, I got a few dollars an hour to read on the job as well as the full discount from the publishers; this meant that, along with Emma Goldman and Flaubert, my self-styled curriculum expanded to include the *I Ching* and the tarot. For years I owned a book called *The Art and Practice of Astral Projection* by someone called Orphiel, though my few efforts to master his instruction never took me anywhere beyond my own hardwood floors. In a used-mystical-book store in San Francisco, I had discovered a battered text entitled *The Book of Venus* that painstakingly explained death and the afterlife; it included shimmering illustrations of the little soul hospitals where we—all of us iridescent blue—recuperated between our earthbound lives. Certainly it could have been worse: I never took the name Rainbow or shaved my head or signed over my paychecks to the Guru Maharaji, all fates that happened to people I knew. I was too much of a dilettante, in revolution and mysticism both, to be a permanent hostage to my passions. Instead I had leftist labor treatises on one bedside table and an astrological ephemeris on the other. I assumed that if dialectical materialism had a grip on the dustbin of history, I could look to Orphiel and the stars to handle the future.

IF THERE WAS ANYTHING CINEMATIC about Mexico in the sixties and seventies, it was the scrub-and-bramble exoticism of *The Wild Bunch,* or maybe, if you got far enough south, the foreboding heat of *The Night of the Iguana.* Except for a couple of

Anglicized resorts and Mexico City, most of the country was not where upright Americans chose to spend their leisure time. Mexico was poor, it could be dangerous, it was stupefyingly beautiful and cheap—all of which made it alluring to the young, restless, and broke. If you could stand up to its adventures, you could live gracefully on a few dollars a day; you might also, if you dared, get a finishing-school education in real life—in American hegemony, the long arm of Catholicism, and Third World poverty. And you could find pockets of uncorrupted natural splendor where all these forces seemed so huge and impersonal as to be rendered meaningless: Pacific coast fishing villages where God could knock you over with a fistful of stars, where you had the illusion, at least for a few minutes a day, that nothing bad ever happened. The country was like some unending Brueghel painting, where the little humiliations and great outrages of the species appeared in equal relief. This was the Mexico where Tennessee Williams had gone to write *A Streetcar Named Desire;* it was Graham Greene's Mexico, too, bleached and quiet and full of menace and awe. I was humanized in Mexico, which is to say radicalized, in part because I went there with no guide and no agenda and only a rudimentary grasp of the language—handicaps and gifts that made me work for every interaction and cherish the ones that took. I saw women begging on the streets of Guadalajara outside the churches, their infants wrapped in their tremendous shawls, and I sat in the back of a cathedral and listened to a noon mass in Spanish, and then I gave my pesos not to the collection plate but to the women, still waiting, on the stoop outside. I learned to eat things I had never seen or smelled and be grateful for them, and I learned early on the Spanish words for *danger, slow,* and *rum and quinine water,* and most important, how to be frightened and lonely in a foreign country, which of course is an education, sometimes profound, in stamina and faith.

My maiden voyage was in 1971, when three other women and I piled into an old Rambler station wagon and headed through the up-country of Mexico toward its southwestern shores. We had among us a few hundred dollars, a flute, a guitar, four backpacks, and a tent, and we drove through ferociously poor and sometimes pastoral places without any destination. Although we never bothered to articulate it, we went to Mexico because we could, and also, in part, because we dared. For all the purported license of the period, women didn't yet travel alone or in packs, and when they did, it wasn't to places like Mexico, a bastion of religious patriarchy where the casual freedoms of *norteamericanas* might be misinterpreted. We made it to Aguascalientes, then Guadalajara, and someone told us about a tiny village called Ajijic, on the shore of Lake Chapala. Later I would hear the stories about the artists and expatriates who had claimed the place: This was where Tennessee Williams supposedly ran a nightly poker game, where Somerset Maugham had finished *The Razor's Edge.* We pitched the tent and camped on the beach, wandering into the village for *café con leche* in the mornings, or to buy fruit and tortillas in the town square. But mostly we clung to our little gringo corner of the lagoon, where we ate papayas and played music, and where my primitive Spanish turned out to be more dangerous than none at all.

We had been in Ajijic long enough to attract the attention of the fishermen who went out on their boats at dawn, and one morning a young man stuck his head inside the tent. My friends had already walked into the village, so I was alone and still sleeping, and I opened my eyes to a stranger smiling at me and saying, *"Buenos días, señorita!"* I sat up in my bedroll and said, with all the authority a sleepy twenty-year-old could muster, what I thought was the word for *go away: "Vamanos!"* He nodded and grinned and said, *"Sí, vamanos!"* Then I yelled it—*"VAMANOS!"*— and he started to look puzzled, if still enthusiastic. I had no idea that I had mixed up my verbs, and was actually hollering, "Let's go!" It was only my body language—a raised fist, an expression of horror—that drove him away.

I got smarter over the next few years when I traveled in Mexico, and I learned enough Spanish to make myself clear, and I stopped sleeping on the beaches. But however much I changed within it, Mexico had become a fixed firmament in my reality and imagination, a Tolkienesque realm where the themes of my life were enacted against the majesty of the place. Mexico could be grand and it could be frightening, but it was always vivid— ordinary gestures were writ large and intensified my otherness. I didn't yet know that this was the gift of travel—to inform and sear the open mind—and partly because of my innocence, I took it in like rain. I had found in Mexico a palette far larger than my own misdemeanor dreams, a place where the wild natural beauty and scattershot danger mirrored my desolation but also surpassed it. I think it was there that I first realized I could leave Texas, leave the life that had seemed ordained by the vastness of the state and its culture, and this idea scared me as much as it fed me, but it also let me exhale and then gather my breath.

So the place pulled me back, wily old prophetess, time and again. I took the train south from Calexico, on the California-Mexico border, and I drove through the desolate midlands of central Mexico, and eventually I discovered Barra de Navidad, a then-undeveloped village south of Puerto Vallarta on the Pacific coast. You could find a decent hotel room for a couple of dollars a night, and along the beaches were cabanas and outdoor restaurants where you could sit for hours, reading or watching the sky or waiting for your life to change. At dusk, the waiters would bring platters of *camarones al ajo,* the shrimp hauled in that morning on the fishing boats, and beer with slices of lime, which worked, too, as a mosquito repellent. Nestled within a lush coastal valley at the foot of Jalisco's mountains, Barra de Navidad was a vacation spot for the Mexican upper class, and one day a well-dressed, stately woman at the next table in a café began a conversation, each of us reaching toward the other in our halting foreign tongues. I learned that she was from Guadalajara, the wife of a physician, and when I told her I was from Texas, she frowned. "Ah, Dallas," she said, and shook her head and touched the cross at her neck. "Bang-bang." I frowned and shook my head in return, and put my hand on my heart. I never forgot the morning tutorial she had given me in history and humility, in the value and limits of language. In how much you could say about America and national calamity and personal loss, without ever having to use the words *Kennedy* or *dead* or even *sad*.

• • •• • •

THE MAN WHO WAS MOST OFTEN MY COLLABORATOR in Mexico was someone so dear to me and yet so insistently remote that he managed to stay estranged even from our little culture of estrangement. The first time I saw Richard, he was working the stove in a friend's kitchen and speaking in a fake French accent, which I believe he thought would downplay the evidence that he was a marvelous cook. He was good at a lot of things and usually didn't like to show it, and he possessed such satiny eloquence that he could distract you from anything, including his own gifts. He was a doctoral student in psychology when I met him, a status that set him apart from our mostly disaffected milieu. He had been through the radical psychologists and abandoned them for the humanitarianism of Erik Erikson and Rollo May, and this alliance was my first evidence of the great kindness at his core. But the face he presented to the world was usually enigmatic and aloof. Where most of the men I knew wore long hair and threadbare clothes as the mantle of their alienation, Richard dressed like a man out of a Dashiell Hammett novel: He wore dark, expensive overcoats, beautiful dress shirts, even with blue jeans, and he kept his hair short—a sort of postwar European persona, enhanced by the Sobranie Black and Golds he smoked. Rather than making him a poseur, this exterior both identified and protected him. He looked hip among straights and straight among hipsters, a disparity that pleased him, I think, because it made both men and women treat him with wary respect. His intellect and compassion were shielded behind an ironic disregard, but he had a voice so deep and consoling, especially when he laughed, that your goal in life, when you were with him, was to make him laugh. We were cornerstones in each other's lives for most of a decade, and I loved him as a friend, sometimes more and sometimes less, and I described him in a journal, in 1972, with a line from Leonard Cohen's "The Stranger Song" that we both liked to quote: "He was watching for the card / That is so high and wild / He'll never need to deal another." The lyrics he would have quoted about me, and did, were from Joan Baez's "Diamonds and Rust," which she wrote about Bob Dylan: "Yes the girl on the half-shell / Would keep you unharmed."

He introduced me to the novels of John le Carré and Graham Greene and the sad, snowy beauty of Robert Altman's *McCabe and Mrs. Miller,* and I think part of his love for me came from the knowledge that I assumed life was tragic but had not, as he had, responded with fatalism. Like an image on the canvas that anchors the painting, he was pivotal in the landscape, though I didn't always know it and often fought it when I did; we tend to revise what we have lost, or fix in the firmament what is already gone. We both had other loves and commitments and yet we circled each other for years like wild horses, until one of us would get too close and the other would flee. I woke up one night at two a.m. to find him standing at the foot of my bed with a bottle of Johnnie Walker Black, because, he said, he missed me and wanted to talk. We sat on the bed in the dark and drank his smoky, expensive whiskey and he said to me, resigned and glad, "You know, not all of us are going to make it. But you and I— we're different. We're going to be OK."

That was a couple of years before he called me, desperate, from Paradise Island in the Bahamas, where he had lost all his money in the casinos. ("Where are you calling from?" I asked him, and though he was a little drunk and slightly panicked, he answered, "A booth in the Midwest," another line from "Diamonds and Rust," because he knew it would make me laugh.) The next day I flew to Nassau with the cash he had given me a few weeks earlier for safekeeping. I went to the blackjack tables and won back half his losses, then made him get on the next plane home.

Here is what I have left of him: an antique silk kimono he brought me from Japan. A 24-karat gold and ebony cigarette lighter that I cannot part with, even though I quit smoking fifteen years ago. A card that came with a dozen roses for Valentine's Day in 1984, after we had given up on each other in all kinds of ways. A clip from a photo booth where he is handsome and laughing. A phone message from 1979, taken by a colleague while I was teaching a class, that reads, "Caldwell: Richard called—is having a psychotic episode. Call soon." I kept this note not because it was true, but because I knew it wasn't, and because he could always get my attention.

We found Barra de Navidad together, he and I, after spending days on a train from the tip of Baja and wending our way south. Because there were few Americans in the village, we thought of it as our own, and the people who lived there treated us with enough grace and courtesy to let us suffer the illusion. We would walk down the beach each night at sunset or later, to watch the sky and sometimes to swim, and one night when the moon was gone we went in the water without any forethought. It was late and no one else was on the beach, and there must have been a strong current, because I found myself alone and much farther out than I had meant to go.

I was a strong swimmer, and even in those reckless days a fairly cautious one, though my tolerance for danger had never been tested so severely, at least in the water. When I saw how far off course I had been carried, I rolled onto my back and began swimming parallel to the shoreline. I had no idea that this was the right thing to do in a riptide, and I have no memory of being afraid. Instead I remember floating in the dark, seeing the sky and the soft glow from the lights of the village, and thinking, *All right, so maybe this is it.* I tried to slow my breaths and kept swimming, looking up at the stars to calm myself, and then I saw Richard running on the beach, and realized I was heading in toward shore.

The next night, wrapped in a towel on the beach at dusk, I thought about that black dance in the ocean and how careless I'd been, or at least how unconcerned. I still wasn't frightened by my close call, though Richard had been and was, but neither did I feel invincible. Something more diffuse had reached out to me, like those signaling lights from town, and that evening I knew, with the near-godlike certainty of the very young, that I would have a different life from any prescribed or anticipated version I had once conceived. That, as Richard had told me back in Texas, I was going to be OK. This realization filled me with sadness, a reaction that confused me at the time but did not weaken my conviction. I had yet to understand that striking out for the territory is inherently a sad enterprise, though the fact is often neglected in the adventure tales we tell ourselves. It is always hard to leave: a home, a drama, a way of life, a life. So I sat there warm and safe that night, held by the sea and a good man and my own good fortune, victim and witness to all the transitory sweetness, like Gatsby's dreams, that stood before and behind me.

RICHARD DIED IN A HOTEL ROOM in Copenhagen in 1991, when he was forty-four, when life had begun to seem too mean and unrelenting for him to stay at it. He swallowed pills to ease this suffering and to quiet what I had always known was his cruel chorus of despair. I later heard that he had given away all his possessions before leaving Texas for Europe, a stripping away that suggested the thoroughness of his plan, as well as the usual care. He had gone far into the long night of a Danish winter to finish his deed, and this, too, broke my heart and seemed in keeping with the dark prince I had known and loved. I sent red roses and white calla lilies to the funeral, the roses for us and the lilies for the pain, and he still comes to see me in my dreams.

Chapter Six

LEAVING MEXICO ALWAYS EXACTED A PAYBACK when you headed through the north country: You had to trade in the surreal ease of the place for the disorientation of the borderlands, where it was clear that the streamlined coolness of America had moved on fast ahead of you. Usually this cultural exchange was fairly straightforward, however shocking, like jumping from a cantering horse onto a moving train. But occasionally something would happen that gave you a sense of the time-space continuum we call history, and how small your place within it. One winter when friends and I were recovering from a bad case of the flu, we stopped for a few days in Mérida, where we amused ourselves by going to see *The Godfather* with a dubbed-in Spanish voice track. We had been away from the States for only a few weeks, but we had been far in the south, without benefit of news or phone communication. When we hit the Texas border, we stopped at the first place we could for a newspaper, and we learned that Lyndon Baines Johnson had died the day before. He had been gone from office for four years. He was only sixty-four at the time of his death, but he looked much older—all the world had watched that craggy face fall from stoic to defeated during his final term. The paper must have been from San Antonio or somewhere in south

Texas. Johnson had been and always would be a Texan first, and the huge headlines mourned his passing to a degree befitting a homeboy who'd grown up to be president. Other stories had been relegated to second place that day, and there on the front page, below the fold, was a headline so subdued and dispassionate that it seemed unthinkable: WAR IN VIETNAM TO END.

It was late January in 1973, and Johnson's death had come near the end of the Paris peace accords, in which the United States had agreed to a cease-fire and troop withdrawal, though the full dismantling of the war effort would take another two years. Still, that small-font declaration, buried as it was beneath the coverage of the death of a former president, took on the unreal hues of something out of *The Twilight Zone*. We had stepped back into America's sunlight to find that the world had shifted— as though all the ghostly, gaseous enemies you'd fought or defined yourself against had simply up and disappeared.

Is it ever possible to locate that crystalline moment, that split in perception, when the story line changes forever? Faulkner claimed that the entire gorgeous canvas of *The Sound and the Fury* had revealed itself in one such flash, when he saw Caddy as a little girl, hanging in her muddy drawers from a pear tree. The image is more exquisite in context: The child in her disheveled purity, trying to look inside the window at her grandmother's corpse, would anticipate, then signify, one of the great family stories of literature, where innocence is no match for the one-two punch of doom and depravity. The story is always supposed to sanction its images. But the image is what contains and sets flight to the story, for all of us, in every narrative we tell—every lie and every sermon—to make sense of the world. It is Saint Joan on the bridge, Peter in the garden at Gethsemane, Hamlet railing in the night alone. It is the snapshot found in a soldier's breast pocket, or the locket photo that opens a million doors of memory.

The visual memory I carry about the Vietnam War is a pixel image, a fitting signifier for a living-room war, and it is the grim infinity of body bags coming off the military cargo planes. Now the picture is as common and as bleached of meaning as a rock video or a beer commercial; that is what media saturation and technology can do to war. But nearly four decades ago, at the height of the Vietnam War, the news footage that captured it— captured the losses, the casualties, the daily grind of fear and horror—was a hieroglyphics of death. Each war invents its own visual language: the peach trees at Shiloh, the trenches at Verdun, the beachheads of Normandy. The glorious mess of Vietnam, so exotic and fecund and wrong, gave us a jazzed-up lexicon of mystery and carnage. A firefight alongside the ragged refrains of "Riders on the Storm." The Hueys and the lime-bleached enemy corpses and the mordant Agent Orange slogans: *Only you can prevent forests.* A marine with an M16 and eyes that had gone on long-range recon patrol, and stayed.

The amazing thing was that all this happened—streamed into our living rooms and onto the screens of our consciousness—on the heels of *Bewitched* and *Father Knows Best.* It seems now, in history's refraction, that you could look up and see Captain Kangaroo on the little black-and-white screen you sat cross-legged before, only to have that ingenuous face give way to the likes of *M*A*S*H*. And that transition may hold another truth about the war, or rather what it meant for the children who came of age watching it, seeing it spliced in between medical dramas and football games. We were the kids of patriotic veterans, we were safe in the suburbs, or so we believed, we were wrapped in the flag long before we set it on fire. We were, for a little while, Caddy in the pear tree, voyeuristic and innocent at once, hell-bent on understanding death.

The body bags came off the cargo planes like auto parts from the line in Detroit. The screen had gotten bigger since Captain Kangaroo and the riderless black horse bearing the caisson at John F. Kennedy's funeral; it had gone to color, but the body bags were black and there were so many of them, one kid after another. Of course not so many after all, if you believe that death can be measured in kill ratios and collateral damages: some sixty thousand on the Wall at the Vietnam Veterans Memorial, hardly anything for a war so long, when nineteen thousand British soldiers had died the first day at the Battle of the Somme. So my hatred of that war is all mixed up, colliding with other numbers whose mothers mourned them in other wars, and other names that stood for terror and the desolate futility never mentioned in the manuals: Ypres and Château-Thierry and Hamburger Hill. And some pathway in the brain, some connector between memory and sorrow, has joined my young loathing of the war in Vietnam with the images that first instructed me—a neural handshake of history and tears that holds, in color, the endless, colorless line of nonviewable remains, once boys and men, on their way back home.

WHAT WOULD MY FATHER HAVE DONE had he been given sons instead of daughters? The question is not new to me but scares me still, because I believe he would have been adamant about the war, even if it meant going there to fight, and so the ruin would have been greater or the fissure less reparable. But I cannot know any of this, any more than I can transplant my own pacifism into the boy I never was. I know, though, that the war in Vietnam hurt my father and me, divided us for years, became an argument that we flung at each other like sand in the eyes, and I don't think we could have borne much more hurt between us. One Christmas I went home from college wearing an old army jacket, and he came into my room that evening, before company appeared, and asked me not to bring up the war in front of guests. I walked out into the den an hour later and sat down on the couch, smiling and companionable, and said, "Did anyone watch the news today? Do we know how many guys we lost in Vietnam?"

My spatial recollection of this has changed over the decades, as the angle of memory will, and now, hovering there as the omniscient narrator of my past, I look down into that warm den with the fire blazing and see how young and infuriating I must have seemed. And how disconcerting: What were upright, God-fearing Texans in the middle of wheat-field America supposed to do with this angry progeny? Some of the credit was theirs; they had given me the curiosity and courage to find out what I felt and then defend it. They had watched me go down that path in the forest, where my sister first led me: toward Old Yeller and the Yearling, on to Joan of Arc on the battlefield and to so many weary soldiers of the imagination, moving down the line. Few routes are so straightforward; otherwise every reader in the world would be a pacifist. Still, I know that my emotional response to war, once I was old enough to hone it into something beyond a child's heartache, began with the bond I felt with my fictional soldiers. This excess of sensibility, as Jane Austen would so kindly define it, could be lavishly sentimental: For too many years I believed there was something inherently heroic about having your guts water the soil of no-man's-land, that behind every soldier who served was a noble half-savage or wounded saint and behind every man who didn't stood a moral victor. My brush took wide strokes in absolving young men from the horrors of combat, whether they were heading for Montreal or the Ia Drang, and I saved my fury for the architects of the war—the cynics who knew what we were doing there, and what we couldn't do, and kept ordering us to do it nonetheless.

But hating a war does not preclude a dark fascination with it, and I have to wonder if the romanticization of Vietnam, mine and everyone else's, was just the underbelly of patriotism—if my concern for every soldier and the prepackaged hell they found incountry was a mantle for something more shadow-bound, which is to say more human. If Vietnam was the great metaphor for my generation, it was not only because it offered a stage of Conradian proportion. Geographically and strategically and even morally, the old rules of engagement no longer held. In a war zone bound by mist and promise, every stranger on the road could be the enemy; opium was easier to get than a full night's sleep. Vets would tell you, coming back, how complex the head trips and how mean those images could make the guilt, but this was not a story that ran on the wires; this was not the narrative that preachers or mothers or even activists wanted to hear. Resting there in the middle of a thousand years of Buddhism and a thousand years of blood feuds, Vietnam looked like the meeting place for God and death in equal measure, a world where good and evil stepped off the plank into some kind of muck that held elements of both. Some men went and couldn't come home again, too many adrenaline rushes and too much insight, peacetime promising only a more drawn-out misery. My Lai was an atrocity, but it was not unique, and that bad news started to explain something else about the war: the random violence unleashed when battle lines were drawn by sniper fire and night raids you couldn't see. If a guy on patrol was just a boy from Georgia praying to his Methodist God, how crazy was it going to make him when the girl he tried to save turned out to be Charlie's sister? Vietnam was a vortex of this sort of relativism, where every aggressive impulse of man had its real-time counterpart that would go you one worse. The helmets said BORN TO KILL and the saying was a salve and a shield, because sometimes the dreams inside those helmets were so bad and so scared they needed somebody to stand up for them, or at least give them a reason for existing. Lost to headquarters, indeed.

I HAVE AN OLD PHOTOGRAPH, taken in 1971 by a photographer
for a local paper, of me flanking one of the huge antiwar marches
to the state capitol in Austin. I was working with a coalition that
included students and socialists and Quakers and Vietnam vets,
and I had volunteered to be a marshal for the march—one of
dozens who kept the crowds in line, watched out for tear gas,
and tried to adhere to the rules of the parade permit we'd been
issued. I have kept this photo not just because it captured a moment in history, at least my history, but because the image of that
girl in her black armband and kohl eye makeup holds everything
I was on my way to being. I look sad and determined and a little
angry, all good qualities for a young woman against the war. The
armband was what identified me to the crowds as a marshal, and
now I attach a poignant, slightly comic quality to my somber
competence, stationed there along my route with the intensity of
a border collie in charge of her flock. The stance—the khaki
army shirt, the accented eyes—is half guts and half glamour, and
my tough-girl façade must have been what the Vietnam vet saw
when I met him later that day, while I was working at a draft-
counseling table on the capitol grounds. He was a big, burly man
with a kind voice, and he looked me over and then asked something no one else ever had, half laughing as he spoke: "What's a
chick like you doing here, trying to counsel guys against the
draft?"

He wasn't so much dismissive as curious, and I liked him

for his bluntness, and thirty years later I like the question still, though in some ways it exposed me and my secondhand dreams and firefights for what they were. Most of the men I knew had found a way out of the draft—Richard's best friend had shown up for his physical wearing a dress, his long black hair curled into gorgeous tresses, and flirted with the intake sergeant before they sent him packing with a permanent deferment. Bad backs and flat feet and a fondness for other soldiers were equally desirable findings for men who didn't want to leave for Canada, and I had friends who'd claimed them all in their efforts for 4-F status. I knew fewer men who had been to Vietnam and returned, and most of those were active in veterans' groups against the war. No one close to me had died there. If the veteran's question was confrontational, it also made me sharpen the sentiments behind the generic outrage I shared with my friends. Self-conscious and unnerved, I blurted out something like "I hate the war; we shouldn't be there; I want to help." A man we both knew, active in VVAW, was working alongside us at the tables, and he saw me floundering and gave us a proper introduction.

Our exchange that day was straightforward, defining as it did the span between personal compassion and moral conviction. But I have remembered it for the broadening world it signaled, when I was on the verge of understanding that feminism and humanism might be the same thing. The vet was a realist: I would never see active duty or even face the choice, so how dare I presume to advise a kid with a low draft number? But I suspect he was also trying to smoke me out as a Cherry Ames do-gooder, one of the overnight-savior girls for whom the rough-hewn veterans' groups had little affection. He needn't have worried. Despite my propensity for sinner-saints over the years, I was too self-involved to be much of a martyr or a caretaker. I identified less with the Melanie Wilkes prototype than with, say, Lady Brett, whose idea of saving the wounded was to seduce them. Not that either literary role model got at the whole truth. The better answer lay as far back as Aristophanes' *Lysistrata,* where the bedroom door slams in the returning warrior's face. I was simply joining the queue of women throughout the ages who understood the claims and casualties of war, and who thought it their subversive duty to protect one group of men from another. This, along with my euphoric, shortsighted sense of history, is what made me shimmy up trees to hang STOP THE WAR banners where they weren't supposed to be; this is what made us pour fake blood on draft files and what made us, me and a million or so more, so earnest and dangerous and triumphant at once.

But the women, not their thwarted soldier-lovers, are the ones we remember in *Lysistrata,* and this focus partly explains why I fixed on the veteran's question, which anticipated my own gravitational shift. It was impossible to live through the activism of the sixties and seventies without realizing the prisms of light each round of illumination had shed upon the others. You couldn't hate the war in Vietnam without seeing the racial components of the draft as well as of the war; you couldn't go on a voter registration drive in Alabama blind to the raw poverty underneath the provincialism of the rural South. One toppling begat another:

When the entire structure was faulty, why bother defending one wing of the house? So if you were a young woman who had come of age with the pill but who had yet to feel the victories of Title IX or *Roe* v. *Wade* or being able to walk down a street alone, you came up against questions like my veteran's all the time. It was innocent but presumptuous, a politically acceptable catcall, a hipster variation on the old What's-a-nice-girl-like-you-doing-in-a-place-like-this, and Black Panther Stokely Carmichael believed he had already answered the question a few years earlier, when he had infamously stated that the correct position for women in the movement was prone.

Carmichael's comment antagonized legions of women who'd spent years on voter registration drives and in antiwar marches, and it was in keeping with an arrogance widespread among the left in those years. Our little mecca was not immune to such assumptions; there were plenty of Texas men with antiwar credentials and shoulder-length hair who expected their girlfriends to have dinner on the table at the end of a hard day on the front lines. But Austin also had its share of steel-spined women whose ancestry included pioneers and sharpshooters, and by the end of the decade, they would have blown open a lot of myths about women in this country forever.

Like all grand-scale dramas, this one started with a lot of smaller, unconnected portraits: a woman in her cloistered study, a pissed-off housewife in her kitchen, a girl at the library with her head in a book. The scholar couldn't get a job, the housewife hated to cook and couldn't talk to her husband, the girl in the library wanted—well, she didn't know what, exactly. She just wanted, which in itself was suspect beyond a certain cauterized desire. And then all these women, so alone with their solitary narratives, put a name to their disaffection or revealed a confidence or read something that changed them—maybe a story as seemingly tame and polite as *Sense and Sensibility,* where the toughest characters in that two-hundred-year-old novel are evicted from their home for being female. Sometimes the book was less transcendent but more prescriptive, like *The Second Sex* or *The Female Eunuch,* even if it would be ignored a decade or two later. The changes were incremental; the changes were profound. Maybe the woman in the kitchen abandoned her post, or maybe she just stood a little taller; maybe the girl in the library grew up and became the woman in the study. Feminism took a lot of dreams that had been corralled into the dictates of marriage or motherhood or second-tier jobs and told us we could do whatever we chose. Anyone who thinks this was an uprising confined to boardrooms or backpacks should have seen a bunch of long-haired, shirtless women on a beach playing drums before a bonfire. Anyone who thinks this was a middle-class, white revolution should count the numbers of children saved or women protected, economically and physically, by activists who split the cocoon and went into law, academe, and social policy. And anyone who needs a picture of what life was like for women before this incandescent explosion need go back only so far as Sylvia Plath's "The Applicant," written in the last months before she killed herself in 1963. "A living doll, everywhere you look, / It can sew, it can cook, / It can talk, talk, talk." If Simone de Beauvoir had told us how to walk away from the kitchen, Plath had left instructions for how to set it on fire.

My first exposure to the women's movement was in 1971, within a few months of that veteran's friendly interrogation. I was walking past a campus rally one afternoon and saw an attractive, black-haired woman in sunglasses commanding the mike. She would become a good friend of mine, but that day, listening to Yannie work the crowd, I was chagrined at how *loud* she seemed. She was pretty, she was articulate, but most of all she sounded fearless, which in itself was a shock. Yannie belonged to a throng of women I would meet in the next few years who were more intrepid than any role model I'd ever known, or at least had yet recognized. They were car mechanics and ex–rodeo stars; they were preachers' daughters, piano players, and judo black belts. Each of them could claim sovereignty over her own life, and that was as much of a marvel thirty years ago as it is a presupposition today.

As for me—well, what would Yannie have seen that day, had she been looking at the nineteen-year-old, barefoot and in old army fatigues, who stood at the edge of the rally, listening to her rail for women's rights? I was a smart, dreamy, estranged young woman who knew enough to hate a war halfway across the globe but not enough to pick a major. I could voice the party line on the history of the Vietnamese people's struggle for independence, but I had yet to read Virginia Woolf and I'd never heard of Mary Wollstonecraft or *A Vindication of the Rights of Woman,* written two centuries earlier. I assumed George Eliot was a man. I had fired a gun—heck, I was a Texan, and my dad hunted birds—but nobody was more weak-kneed than I when it came to romance. If that was the year I would swoon under the trashy allure of *The Bell Jar*, just published posthumously in America, I was still a long way from experiencing the white-hot rage and terror of Plath's *Ariel.* I'd been hearing and reading about tragic women for as long as I could remember, but I hadn't yet figured out that the tragedies were often man-made, and what usually defined the fallen hero-ines. Instead I had learned too well these tacit themes, granting the inevitability of sorrow or madness in a woman's life. I could see Tess there on the moors, desolate heiress to her own passion, and I knew that pious women, too, suffered in spite of their piety, without claim even to Tess's brief freedom or Anna Karenina's flicker of joy. I'd heard myriad stories about female strength and trouble in my own family, women who'd been caretakers and cor-nerstones, or women who had stumbled on what seemed a fated path. But I couldn't have traced the line then, I couldn't have named the sorrow or, more important, gone to its headwaters, and God knows I wouldn't have known how to redirect the flow. I was, in other words, like a lot of other potential converts at Yannie's feet that day, vaguely aware that something was wrong and that she was right, and stunned that she had the audacity to say it.

She would embarrass me often over the next few years, usu-ally for daring to do what I would not, though once only for play-ing her guitar while camped out at a terminal at the San Francisco airport. (My discomfort touches me in retrospect, because it seems like a flag for a deeper fear, and I know now that fear is usually the precursor to change, and the women's movement changed me wholly, or maybe just let me find out who I already was.) For all its tributaries and long-range consequences, the earliest effect of feminism was a widening of spirit, which meant simply that you burst through the margins of a preordained life: You went to Mexico in a beat-up Rambler, or hung Mother Jones posters next to the ones of Che, or moved to Taos to live in a yurt. You founded a women's health clinic; you went to law school; you did or didn't want kids but could have cared less about getting married. Some of these left turns and self-discoveries would last a lifetime, though there were plenty of transient misfires and comic extremes. I have a fond memory of a sheep-shearing workshop, earnest in tone and heavily attended, at a women's festival in Mendocino County, California. Two volunteers from a feminist farm collective demonstrated on one of their own, and the sheep stood there, mid–buzz cut, with all the stately patience of a nude model. Not everyone was convinced that, come the revolution, the skill would be essential; a few of us sneaked off, took mescaline, and went to stare at the Russian River instead.

The antics of Austin's feminist tribe tended more toward the outrageous and theatrical than the merely radical; something about Texas itself—all that space and heat and self-aggrandizing history—had given rise to a sisterhood blessed with flint and muscle. Not for us the wilting flowers of Dixie or the upright bluestocking tradition of the Northeast. Our foremothers had calluses on their hands and a rifle slung across their backs; their legendary courage would go a long way in helping us take on the six-gun patriarchy. We had the oldest whorehouse in America (the notorious Chicken Ranch), the first women's drill team (the Kilgore Rangerettes), and legends from Babe Didrikson to Bonnie Parker in our halls of fame and infamy. Janis Joplin had crawled out of Port Arthur all the way to rock 'n' roll heaven, the essence of little-girl dreams become grit-and-glory realities. We had stamina and occasional virtuosity and a grand sense of the absurd; standing on that patch of heaven overlooking the rest of our lives, we believed we could get anywhere we tried.

By the time I got to the campus mall that day in 1971, most of my life had been lived within or despite the strictures of men's desires and expectations. I had shone under their praise, wavered under their criticism, followed the paths they laid out or turned away in exasperated or quiet defiance. Even my worst rebellions had men posted at either end of the route: Suffer the calculus professor but wither under a boyfriend's judgment, hurt the father but please the vet. I cared tremendously what all of them thought, no matter how grave or daring my detour from their instruction. I even cared that day I stood listening to Yannie, alert to her words but flinching under the gaze of the men walking past. And then, with the natural diffusion of water, my life began to map its own course. For all its external conflagrations, the women's movement gave us something that couldn't be legislated, condemned, or ever taken away: some core balancing point, a plié that sheltered and enhanced the spirit. And this, more than anything else, was the movement's seminal legacy and greatest threat. Feminism redirected the narrative. It was when the story, for a million protagonists, finally stopped being about somebody else.

⸰⸰⸰⸰⸰

THE SOEUR QUEENS were an all-girl honky-tonk band started in 1971 by a gifted lunatic from east Texas named C.J. The band's name was taken from the French noun for *sister*, but its double entendre (in Texas, you'd just say *sewer*) was testament to what kind of band we were. C.J. played guitar, wrote most of the songs, and provided the élan vital for the group; we also had a Czech-American piano player with a guttural alto so sultry she could set a dance hall on fire, a bass player, a couple of backup guitarists, and myriad vocalists, not all of whom could carry a tune. I played the flute, which is a merciful way of saying I tried, and I sang the occasional duet with a godsent soprano who left us, wisely, to play with Butch Hancock and eventually form her own zydeco band. We performed at fund-raisers and barbecues and back-alley juke joints like the One Knite, where a fight broke out late one evening when somebody threw a chair. We enlivened any crowd just because we'd show up, fearless, and sing "Austin Uptown Down" or "The Only Sin Is Frettin' " or Jimmie Gilmore's "Dallas." The talent in the group carried the rest of us: The fundamental requirement for being a Soeur Queen, more than musical skill, was attitude. *The Soeur Queen Songbook*, which we self-published in the mid-1970s, carried this lowercase inscription: "this songbook is dedicated to all those everywhere

who are soeur queens in their minds. those of us who put it together were obviously out of ours."

That dedication wasn't much of a legal defense, but it might
have been the only one available, had we not gotten out of Houston when we did. One winter weekend in 1973, most of the band
and a few extras piled into a couple of vans and drove down to
Houston for the National Women's Political Convention, being
held at the Rice Hotel. Whether anyone else knew it yet or not,
we assumed our presence would be required. After we'd seen the
conference itinerary, full of grim plenary sessions and actual
work, someone in our ragtag coalition suggested that the Soeur
Queens kidnap Gloria Steinem. This was obviously more delu-
sion than strategy; it was just that the NWPC agenda looked staid
and bourgeois, and we imagined ourselves part of the entertain-
ment. Like most moments of Soeur-Queen-inspired folly, the
plot was short-lived, though a few of us did go so far as to join
Steinem in an elevator and serenade her with "Glo-o-o-o-o-o-o-
r-r-i-a, in excelsis deo." We were warming up for the two-minute
concert we gave onstage the first morning of the convention. I
don't remember what we sang—probably "Private Property," or
"Custom Made Woman Blues," or maybe Yannie or C.J. had
written something special for the occasion. But we were thrown
off the stage halfway through the song, and one humorless net-
work cameraman chided us for being troublemakers. A better
piece of criticism came from the mother of one of the Soeur
Queens, a middle-aged liberal Democrat who was in the audience. Once we had gotten the hook, she followed us and our pha-

lange of security guards to the lobby outside the auditorium, where we had been escorted. She hugged her daughter, then beheld the rest of us as though we had just performed at halftime at the Cotton Bowl. "Y'all are the worst band I've ever heard!" she said brightly; we took it for the matchless praise it was.

Guerrilla high jinks like ours were happening all over the country in those days, too often misinterpreted by media coverage or by the targets we sought to disrupt. Beyond the youthful lunacy was an effort to shake up the status quo and ask for more—to widen the scope of the women's movement beyond the borders of preordained acceptable behavior. So whether we were spray-painting buildings or starting food co-ops, the point was transformation: stopping the war, changing the world, saving something beyond our own skins. The cost of our idealism was the fuel it took; we didn't know then, couldn't have borne knowing, that most forms of deliverance carry a caveat of impermanence. A lot of us faltered or crashed when we realized that, when we saw that hope wasn't infinite or unconditional, and that we would have to save ourselves. Some of what happened was the inevitable breakthrough to adulthood, when you land, unscathed, and see that not everybody made it. Then you must go on, as Beckett's narrator insists, and so you go on.

We went on to softer climes: medical school, motherhood, social advocacy jobs. A few people went to jail, or to alternative meccas hidden in the landscape across the country, or to some obscurity more subdued and saner than what we had shared. But then true stories always end with asterisks, with finessed dreams or rag-and-bone choices that take you somewhere other than where you intended. The trick is to let a time like ours shape you utterly without its becoming the apex of your life. The trick is to relinquish the drama and walk out of the fire, burnished and whole, and hold on to its legacies without looking back. Otherwise you fall prey to your own brilliant possibility; you become Updike's Rabbit Angstrom, muddling along in your melancholia, married first and always to the amber past.

MOST OF THE BEDLAM AND HEARTACHE that attended those years unfolded against a public backdrop; whether your trouble was a drug problem or tear gas in the face, you could attribute some of it to the times in which we lived. Two casualties I witnessed seemed to possess this sense of magnified resonance, as though the earth itself were shifting and precarious. These were crashes, I know now, that probably would have happened with or without revolutions or Day-Glo sentiments. But at the time they were precursors to an end we couldn't yet see: They were the canaries in the mine.

The first was the collapse of a tender girl I knew during my first year in Austin, who lived down the hall from me in off-campus housing. Marla was my antiwar Quaker friend's roommate, and everyone who knew her marveled at her unwavering powers of concentration. She was a straight-A psychology major on her way to graduate school; in the midst of campus upheaval and a gaggle of mercurial girls, Marla held steady to the course.

The first signs of her unraveling were mild—disconnected conversation, staring too long into space—and we attributed these lapses to exam pressures. Unlike most of the girls on the wing, Marla didn't drink or do drugs, and seemed to measure low on the scale of self-inflicted wrongs.

Then she got worse. She stopped eating, she stopped sleeping, and eventually she stopped speaking. Valiantly and stupidly, we tried to help her ourselves. We spoke softly, we brought her food, we smiled and fretted. Her roommate and I went over to the main drag to buy a book we knew she wanted, *Gandhi's Truth: On the Origins of Militant Nonviolence,* by Erik Erikson. I remember holding the book on my lap and sitting next to Marla on her bed, talking to her and stroking her arm, though by then she gave no sign that she knew I was there. We finally had the sense to get the resident manager; by that evening, Marla's parents had arrived. They took her home the next morning, and we found out later, after she had been withdrawn from classes, that she had suffered a similar break two years earlier. With a callowness I hope was youth, I wondered for months if she had kept the Erikson book, or if she had ever recognized the intended kindness of our gesture.

What I was really pondering, though, was whether my little token, my sacrifice presented to implacable gods, had penetrated the dark mist of where Marla had gone—if I had helped, at all. Somewhere I knew that I hadn't, and I couldn't abide this inconsequence. Because of where I grew up and because of my own brooding nature, I had long had a sense of my limits and limitations: All that sky and introspection allowed for a fair amount of ennui. But there was also enough Calvinist pluck in my heritage for me to believe that most evils of life could be fought and overcome, or at least pierced. I was too young to have yet beheld the random, private terrors that could afflict someone of my generation, someone as kind and unblemished as Marla. Worse, the curative pouch I had believed in and carried with me all these years had failed. No words had reached her and no sacred text could help, even when we had laid it at her feet.

A few years later I faced a starker encounter with the ravages of the psyche, more emphatic in convincing me of what I could and couldn't do. I was a volunteer at Womenspace, the peer counseling center that friends of mine had founded, and I had been through what was considered adequate training to handle most walk-in cases. The problems we saw tended to be acute and relatively mild: transient depression, relationship or situational anxieties. Because we were open until ten p.m. and housed across the main drag from campus, we got a number of female students who needed help but didn't want to go to UT psych services or didn't qualify as an emergency. The first time I met Karen, I assumed she belonged in this category; she was under the care of a university psychiatrist, she told me, but it was evening, she was lonely and having trouble sleeping. She had a frail intensity that made me reach out to her, and my warmth must have shown, because after that night, Karen came back to Womenspace often and refused to see anyone but me. Rather than noting this as the red flag it was, I responded by shifting my schedule to accommodate her; I was touched and wrongly flattered by her need, though at least I had the sense to find out the name of her doctor. Within a couple of weeks, she seemed to improve: Where before she had seemed bowed by sadness, now she was bright-eyed and smiling. Then she came in one evening and sat down with treacherous calm. "I've stopped taking my Stelazine," she told me, and the hair stood up on the back of my neck. "And today I bought a gun."

I knew Stelazine was a commonly prescribed antipsychotic; what I didn't know was that Karen had been on it, or that she had been diagnosed with schizophrenia. I tried not to stare at the leather bag she was guarding on her lap, which I thought might well hold my immediate fate. Then I got up from my chair, asked if she wanted some water, and went next door and called her psychiatrist, who was as steady and unerring as a compass in a hurricane. (He was also furious with me, I think, for having the temerity to treat someone so sick, but he had the sense to mask this fury and attend to Karen.) After a three-minute conversation between doctor and patient, she had given me the leather bag, the psychiatrist was on his way to our offices, and Karen was headed for the hospital. The gun, which had not been loaded, was disposed of by the police. Karen had capitulated immediately—she seemed grateful for the call to her doctor, and hugged me before she left. Impressed by my coolness under fire, I went home giddy with relief, until I got scared a few hours later, when I let myself feel how catastrophic the night might have been.

The Karen affair, as I came to consider it, humbled me enough to put an end to my naïve arrogance, at least when it came to impersonating a mental health professional. But it also spoke to some greater meltdown, some impotence and chaos in the culture, and I think this parallel was what intensified its effect on me. The world we had tried so hard to claim and tame had proved as dangerous as ever, its utopian light waves giving way to the usual muddle as well as a post-Watergate nihilism. California's ephemeral Eden had been overrun by the terror of the Zebra killings; the New Left had disintegrated into splinter factions of old Stalinists or new madmen. In Austin, what had once seemed a lifestyle of liberation now resembled nothing so much as despair and derailment. You didn't have to go far to ascertain this shift, this undercurrent of wary indifference or fear: Behind the inevitable marijuana glaze or rock 'n' roll cool, a look of panic was starting to show in people's eyes. One of Austin's vanguard hell-raisers joined A.A., which few people of my generation had yet considered. Two women I knew decided to marry and have babies, a solution a lot of us found quaint, if effective. I was twenty-six and had been zeitgeist-surfing long enough to be exhausted, though the greater fatigue was from being lost, from trying to make a career out of estrangement. And if my near-crash with Karen had taught me anything, it was that my penchant for tragic heroines was better off indulged when they were imaginary. Intent upon saving my own neglected charge—my mind—I half crept over to the UT campus to see what ruin I had left there five years earlier.

Chapter Seven

IT WAS SUMMER SESSION, and I enrolled in the only class I thought I could tolerate, an interdisciplinary literature course on the postwar beat experience that met every day. My instructor was a tall, soft-spoken man around thirty who liked to quote Bob Dylan, and his reading list zigzagged among Twain, Kerouac, and Frederick Exley. I liked Anderson immediately for his quiet irony and his assumption that what he had to teach us lay mostly in the novels. The chief requirement for the course, he told us, was written feedback; if it was his job to crack the code, ours was to read and to think, then turn in the notes that proved it. His class was cross-listed in both English and American Studies, the latter still a small, maverick field where you could find experts on jazz, baseball, and the sociocultural impact of disease. This sounded like the sort of place where a beached bohemian might find herself, or at least hole up for a while. I smiled over the reading list and resolved to make it through the next six weeks.

The hardest and best passages in my life have tended to arrive in this circumspect fashion, like a tornado knocking on the side door before it levels the land. Most of the things I had accomplished that held—that mattered and lasted—had been feats of near-deluded determination: walking through the early effects of polio, climbing that little papier-mâché mountain at the library, hoisting my heart past the flat resignation of the Panhandle plains. I had tricked and coaxed myself through each long crossing, the insistent superego shepherding the fear within. Now I'd wandered back into these halls with the nonchalant vow that I could bail whenever I chose. Within three months, I had mapped out the rest of an undergraduate degree, taken the graduate school entrance exams, and applied for the doctoral program in American Studies.

What I knew about the field was relatively slight. I knew Tom Wolfe had been trained in the discipline at Yale before descending upon the newsroom of the *New York Herald-Tribune* to churn out his ragtime-piano prose. The UT program, I had also heard, was notorious for sounding hip but being grueling, with two fierce professors guarding its gates like stone lions. There were stories of departmental shenanigans: One middle-aged teacher of literature was known to tap-dance on his seminar table to wake lethargic students. A lead question on a recent Ph.D. orals exam had come from the same man: "Why is *Jaws* a better book than *Moby-Dick*? Defend."

Like so much about American Studies, the question sounded heretical but was brazenly simple: It presented an untruth with insolent ease, expecting its unfortunate recipient to bring an arsenal of English literature and popular culture to expose its fallacy. This dialectic was why I ultimately came to love the field. Where so much of the humanities had become reactive by the 1970s, torching or hacking away at the wheel in order not to reinvent it, American Studies had little precedent to constrict its aims. Its affinities lay with literature and history but were essentially Socratic: hypothesize, discuss, prove. Such notions appealed to a young woman who had run screaming from the recent onslaught of deconstructionist chic. Besides, my time on the road—my five-year sabbatical on the highways and back roads of America—had taught me that human culture was as complex and interdependent as anatomy, its painting or novels no more separable from its wars or moral codes than a vascular system is from a heart. I had seen this hunch confirmed everywhere from Faulkner's South to the bluesy Texas of Leadbelly and Lightnin' Hopkins, and the intuition so informed me by the time I returned to academe that I doubt I could have tolerated any discipline too far removed from its tenets. American Studies, with its right- and left-wing cranks and Pynchon acolytes and tap-dancing madmen, seemed tailored to my own disheveled spirit.

Those first weeks in Anderson's class gave little evidence of the intensity and purpose that would follow. I sat staring out the window, camouflaged behind my rebel-girl credentials but too self-conscious to speak in class. I tended to walk in at the last minute, sprawl in the front row, then feign indifference while Anderson delivered us to Ginsberg or Neal Cassady or other icons of rebellion. When he sparked a discussion, which was often, he would look my way, though less hopefully each day, because I never opened my mouth. That reticence disappeared at night, when I was alone before a typewriter. Where most students delivered the evidence of their reading with a few handwritten paragraphs, I handed in single-spaced treatises, burying them in the midst of the pile so as not to call attention to myself. A day or two later, Anderson would return our comments, usually with a cursory "OK" written in the margin. At the end of my typed manifestos, beneath my hundreds of words, he would have written, in meticulous cursive, a few hundred words in reply.

I lived for the days the words came back. We were having an elemental dialogue, Anderson and I, each charmed by the other's insights, him coaxing me into the light like some feral creature in the woods. I saved the papers for years, as a reminder not that I could write but that I had to, and that something far larger than I had been unleashed. Safe with my German Adler typewriter and my untrained, gamboling opinions, I held forth on Kerouac's bad writing, Exley's misogyny, Dylan's woozy, melancholic genius. No ideologues in sight here: no structuralists or Marxists to bully my impressions. By the end of the summer my teacher and I had traded thousands of words between us, two inflamed minds doing their careful tango, though we had yet to exchange more than a few sentences in person. When I learned near the end of the class that Anderson had taken a job in Maine, I was despondent, and embarrassed by my response. I had the childlike superstition that this new grail of mine, this joy, would go with him.

If the luster of illusion touches all human relationships, what distinguishes the idealized other—the analyst, the teacher, the bartender-lover-priest—is the unalloyed nature of its context. My reliance on Anderson had taken on this hue in part because of its epistolary purity, the usual strength of the student-teacher dyad intensified by our lengthy correspondence. More significant but serendipitous, he happened to be standing there when I fell out of the forest, hungry and searching. Like all good mentors, he knew how to be kind in the shadows, then step out of the way.

My fears about my teacher taking my creativity with him when he left would not last long. If I maintained any belief that the power was beyond me, I let it reside in my electric Adler, which hummed along in loyal communion every time I turned it on. But it was literature itself that offered the fire and freedom of the next few years. Unlike my previous forays into the conventional study of English lit, now I found that my instincts about a novel—about language and the imagination, about the necessary meters of the heart—were stone markers along the road, and that I could trust what I knew and learn what I didn't. The radical transformations I had sought on the streets and highways of America turned out to belong to places of the imagination, beyond the reaches of cant and almost celestially self-contained: Faulkner's Yoknapatawpha, Hardy's Wessex, Eliot's little town of Middlemarch. Here was a realm where the burdens of civilization might be exposed and then transcended. In Hawthorne I found portraits of such stark moral reckoning that my Calvinist ancestors seemed heathens by comparison. I lost myself in the odd, brittle sadnesses of Carson McCullers: she with her tea and sherry and fey sensibility, delivering a South as cockeyed as it was dangerous. Within the temporary fugue state that every reader knows, I traveled much in Concord, as Thoreau said; I dallied in James's country gardens and shivered on the streets of Dickens's London. I was willing to go anywhere with these commanders, so long as they would take me there again.

Before I walked back into Garrison Hall, I had spent the cusp years of my adulthood disillusioned by the institutions that were supposed to be havens. My whirlwinds of intensity would have to wear themselves out before I would consider that Faulkner might have more to offer than, say, "Street Fighting Man," or that setting the mind on fire might be the most defiant and lasting act of all. I had been scared and humbled by Hawthorne's "Wakefield," the story of a man who, mistaking alienation for freedom, walks away from his own life, then spies on it from a block away for twenty years. Wakefield's little odyssey takes him only to a fog-bound limbo, until one day he gives up his self-banishment and returns to all he left behind. Exile is by nature solipsistic: All prodigal sons and daughters must realize, upon going home, that some of what they fled has gone on well without them. I had walked away, too, but whatever dreams I had lost or found, it seemed these shelters of the imagination could not be hurt by my retreat—they stood there still, like so much divine and silent statuary, presuming but not requiring my return. And now, like Wakefield, I had been given the key to get back in.

DESPITE THE ETHEREAL QUALITY of my desires, most of the aid I received in graduate school was of a more practical nature: I survived with the help of Dalmane, cheeseburgers, Winstons, and a small, tensile-strength brunette whose kindness was a cover for her fierce competence. A year older than I, Caitlin Miller had been a pediatric nurse before returning to academe; while I'd been hitchhiking to Berkeley or slinging vegetarian hash, Caitlin was tending to fevers and broken arms, no doubt with the same blend of warmth and unflappable calm that saved her now. Because she had trained in the trenches of medical hierarchies in the 1970s, she knew how to navigate the rough terrain of men in power, and she managed this act with diplomacy and wit. (When men she didn't know approached her, which happened often because of her good looks, she would extend a warm hand and introduce herself as a neurosurgeon. This usually achieved the desired goal, which was to end the conversation.) I met her in a seminar on the history of medicine taught by a crusty, likable scholar who was the only leftist on the faculty, and he had the foresight to see that Miller herself, from her days in the field, was a primary source. She liked my audacity and I liked her good sense; together, we learned how to outlast sadistic faculty members, the terrors of teaching, the monastic deprivation of reading for orals. We shared an office where we smoked and read and cultivated this joint courage. On the first day of teaching my own class, when some thirty undergraduates awaited me down the hall and I stood frozen at the final bell, Miller took the cigarette from my mouth, handed me my syllabus and a Diet Coke, and shoved me out the door. Now I knew how she'd kept all those kids in vaccination clinics from crying.

Those years would turn out to be as daunting, frustrating, and exhilarating as any I had spent on Austin's front lines of rebellion. I learned to think and argue on my feet, endure a three-hour seminar on the Chicago pragmatists, stand up to criminally smart professors who lived for the scent of graduate student fear. Brave before riot police, here I was rendered mute and dry-mouthed when faced with, say, the rise of the federal banking system. Here, my leftish street cred only made me a fledgling recruit for the liberals and catnip for the conservatives. My predictable position was to hold forth on the Wobblies or the class-bound history of birth control, and my teachers tolerated these indignations, partly because I was easy to provoke—they were bored, I think, with the bovine affability of those students who aimed to please. I aimed instead to preach. I began essay exams with such sweeping particularities as "The entire sordid script of American history. . . ." Rather than rising to the bait, my professor, a man named Nash with a tone so dry he could start a brushfire with it, simply replied in the margin, "Don't overdo it."

But I did overdo it, again and again, an excess that allowed the arguments to stay lively. Nash was a historian with a demeanor as severe as his intellect; he wore a Lincolnesque beard and thirty-year-old tweeds, insisting that his students call him "Mister" rather than "Professor," in proper nineteenth-century boarding-school fashion. He refused to go near a television or newspapers, preferring that his vast little world be influenced only by books and scholarly journals. Every student within a half-mile radius of Garrison Hall lived in fear of his disdain, with which he was generous; one poor fellow barely recovered from Nash's scorn over his continued mispronunciation of the names of Proust and

Alfred Stieglitz. What Nash had to offer his charges, assuming one could get past his irascibility and his office door, was a mind of such bracing clarity that it was like swimming in Arctic waters to train for a triathlon. If you could survive his rigors, you could stand up to anything.

Except perhaps his superior, the departmental chair, a man in some ways smarter, funnier, and scarier than Nash, and who was also known for being half insane. This made for a wonderfully patricidal exchange between the two, to the entire department's delight, since their unvarying warfare took some of the heat off everyone else. Roth was a celebrated historian with a fondness for chain-smoking, beer, and whichever female student was smart enough to present a challenge but patient enough to tolerate his drunken-Galahad advances. He thought nothing of adding an extra hour to his already interminable evening seminars, so that you would stagger out at eleven p.m., dumb with fatigue but roused by the virtuoso discourse you had just beheld. He had managed to antagonize half the departments on campus over the years, but he had won enough prizes to ensure him a room with a view wherever he landed. You couldn't get through American Studies without traversing the territories where Nash and Roth reigned. They had divided up their kingdoms with warring ide-ologies and shameless raids, and thus held all of us hostage to their joint review and their egos. No one in his or her right mind tried to survive them simultaneously; the only sound course of action, it was said, was to let one tutorial prepare you for the other. I took them both on at once.

As was so often the case with my acts of bravery, this little daring was a combination of chutzpah and ignorance, but the reasons didn't matter by the time I discovered, with wretched comprehension, what I'd done. More consequential was the unforeseen effect of my dual affections: The two men began duking it out for my allegiance, as though I were Switzerland, or the Louisiana Territory. This had far less to do with my intellectual currency than with the game; I believe they would have fought over anyone standing on the bridge between them. They became the first two readers on my thesis and argued constantly over its merits and weaknesses, to the point that I eventually stopped listening to either one, though I doubt they noticed. When I left the university, the year before I was to take doctoral orals, they even assumed opposite positions as to what fate awaited me. Roth had approached me one afternoon with his version of vinegar-and-pepper affection, tossing something I'd written onto my desk. "Get out of here," he said, with enough gruffness to scare me. Then he grinned that mad, familiar grin. "You need to leave before we ruin you." Nash, on the other hand, belittled me for going. He cursed the investment he'd made, declared me a para-academic (his worst possible insult), and told me I'd be selling pencils on a Cambridge street corner within a year.

Unlike my former vault from ivy-covered watchtowers, this departure would have reason beyond my own confusion: We all three knew, I think, that I hadn't the sensibility of a scholar, or much desire to be one. I was too stubborn and soft at once, preferring metaphor to methodology, and I had long supposed that my academic retreat was a temporary barracks, an outpost at the edge of literature where I could survey its wide horizons. For that considerable instruction, I spent my last year of graduate school immersed in the critics of days past. I read Orwell and Lawrence to understand literature; I read Alfred Kazin and Philip Rahv to understand America. I fell in love with the authoritative brilliance of Edmund Wilson and James Agee, and I thrilled to the bitchy consequence of a young theater critic named Mary McCarthy, the Vassar girl whose dirty novel I'd discovered years before. That she had once been married to Wilson—that she had set a small fire outside his study door to get his attention—well, these crucial and scintillating facts only made her calling as a writer all the more enticing. It was one sort of pipe dream to fancy yourself a young Emerson or Howells; these were not the visions a small-town Texas girl employed, no matter how urbane or radicalized I'd become in the past few years. But a mentor with an armory of opinions, a couple of failed marriages, and a socialist rap sheet? That was a résumé I could aim for, or at least dream about. For all the knowledge gleaned from the giants of critical discourse, it was the bad girls of the profession who told me I could try to be a writer: those loudmouthed broads who smoked and drank their way through New York newsrooms and barrooms, through jobs and divorces, who had dared (as McCarthy did) to write an essay on Wilde called "The Unimportance of Being Oscar"—or to say about Eugene O'Neill, simply and without a backward glance, that the man "cannot write." I had grown up in a tough part of Texas, with tornadoes and jail cells and angry dads, and I knew courage when I saw it, even if it was hidden behind the breast-plate of an old Royal typewriter.

JUST AS THE FOOL FIGURES PROMINENTLY in the tarot and Puck holds the secrets to *A Midsummer Night's Dream,* the tap-dancing madman of Garrison Hall would have his due in show-ing me the break in the hedge. Simmons was an English professor who had wandered into American Studies because, as was the case for most of its faculty, the program's peculiarities mirrored his own. He spoke with the melodious enthusiasms of an Elizabethan actor, but his fractured smile disguised his love of literature and made you think he was making fun of it all—the students, the novels, the entire universe—every time he spoke. His seminars were filled to capacity, both for the guaranteed knowledge within and the anticipated show, and Simmons worked this atmospheric pressure like the performer he was: He once broke into a resounding chorus from the musical *Okla-homa!*—"Oh, the farmer and the cowman should be friends!"—just to make a point about de Crèvecoeur's eighteenth-century classic *Letters from an American Farmer.* During class he ad-dressed each student with formalities—Mr. Peters, Ms. Miller—and yet he could make even courtesy sound ludicrous. It was hard to get and keep your footing in dialogue with the man; the uninitiated couldn't tell if they were being praised or mocked.

My first exposure to his magniloquence came during a semi-nar on major American writers, with a reading list devoted entirely to novels by white men. Because it was the late 1970s, Simmons's curriculum was still standard fare. When a female student questioned his selections at the first class meeting, he obligingly, almost theatrically, added Edith Wharton to the list. He revealed no gender affinities, though, when it came to his students, each of whom he treated, beyond the mordant veneer, with an oddly precious regard. Deviating from the coolness cultivated by most senior faculty, he insisted at the beginning of each term that his charges explain why they were in attendance; if you gave an answer deemed vague or coy, he pressed mercilessly until he got the deeper truth he sought. So it was there that I publicly muttered that I wanted to write—"Yes, Ms. Caldwell, and what, pray tell, do you wish to write?"—and there, too, that he bestowed upon us the splendor of *Light in August,* the cranky reveries of Flannery O'Connor, the manic labyrinths of *Moby-Dick.* Simmons grasped and even applauded the mad sacrifices of creative fire, and he led us through the provinces of literary history as though we were scouts on our first camping expedition, with him our merry leader.

Some days this gusto could be crippling: You could summon only so much vigor about Puritan sensibility or Cooper's Natty Bumppo. But if the class seemed indifferent, Simmons got worse, railing and insisting we share what we knew or intuited. One afternoon he was half swooning in his delivery of the onslaught of modernism, assuming we would join in his homage. His students, glassy-eyed one and all, refused to budge. Where, Simmons implored, can we locate the origins of modernism in the novel? No takers, though it was a standard American Studies question. The silence grew mortifying. Finally I blurted out what half the students must have known. "Uh, *Ulysses,*" I said. "Joyce's use of stream of consciousness." Simmons, of course, had been teaching for decades, and he was hard to rattle—he knew someone would take the bait, would crumple under the discomfort he had spawned. "Yes, Ms. Caldwell!" he cried, grateful but unbowed. "*Take* us there!"

For a couple of years afterward, this became a departmental refrain, the joke summoned whenever anyone needed to know anything. "Take us there, Ms. C.!" And yet I remember it now with something kinder than the amusement we shared at Simmons's expense. He knew, with that simple navigational imperative, that in fact there was somewhere to go—knew that literature was just a world over, like Wakefield's old neighborhood, from our own third dimension, and that it was his task and joy to show us the way.

Simmons's reputation for class antics sometimes obscured the heartfelt teacher he was; in his commentaries on the essays we gave him, his in-class formalities gave way to more intimate monikers. He addressed me in these written notes as Clever Girl, a reversal of my initials but also his friendly nudge that facility was not the answer for a writer—that one could be clever at the expense of anything deeper. Had I any doubt of this barbed-wire-and-honey interpretation, I was reminded of it explicitly several years after I had left Texas, when he sent me a copy of his book on writing that had just been published. Buried there within his fussy discourses on usage were the exact words he had written on one of my essays. He had changed my initial for publication, but not my epithet, and he had included a passage in which he accused me of wiseacre acrobatics. "There is too much cleverness in the world," he quoted himself telling a Ms. R., "and too little truth. Let's try to have more truth."

Rediscovering his advice all this time later, I didn't know which was more impressive: that Simmons would so precisely deliver the lesson I had needed, or that he could be so maniacal in his forethought. The book was proof that he had photocopied all his handwritten responses to students for years on end. So! What we had been getting was a calculated generosity that instructed us and served him. This seemed hilariously in keeping with the tap-dancing Fool—Puck, after all, understands the power of his elixir. But it also told me something invaluable about the writer's soul: Even when dispensing fairy dust, take notes. Clever Man.

My professors, louts and hooligans and unrepentant dreamers all, did what they could with me, their half-lazy, half-clever girl who could never quite make the leap to their shores. We all knew it was becoming hopeless in the last year, when for an entire summer I carried around an unread copy of Eugene Genovese's immense treatise on slavery, *Roll, Jordan, Roll,* deluding myself that I was reading for orals. Roth, in particular, was relieved when I announced that I was taking the last train out. I had always had difficulty feigning scholarly vehemence, and I was lousy at flattering the right people; he feared my impolitic ways would be hell in the job market.

The more crucial reality, though, was that I had learned too well the bliss imparted in that first class with Anderson, in the sultry summer that began this trek. What I had found and could no longer live without was the sweet staccato of my Adler keys, which seemed to say anything I wanted and often far better than I knew I could say it. Every young writer has such epiphanies, when the interior space of the writing life reveals itself and the foundation of the future is laid. For me, I had discovered an edifice within that was stronger and safer than anything I had ever imagined—my own little storm cellar, born in and formed by that Panhandle wind, stocked with calm and crystalline desire. And now that I knew it was there, I could no more turn my back on it than I would have chosen not to breathe.

Not long before I turned in my key to Garrison Hall, before I crated the books and steered the Volvo onto the asphalt headed east, I had an encounter with a visiting scholar from a neighboring department that epitomized my ambivalence about academe— about the misinterpretations it fostered, the little political cadres that helped it to function. In her few months in Austin, the woman had already garnered a reputation for being provocative without cause; she was an advocate of feminist theory, but her position was more polemical than creative. I was neither friend nor foe to academic factions; my years in Austin's flea-market politics had taught me to keep my head and never put my alliances up for sale. What

I loved about the women's movement storming the universities was the same richness that had helped to open up my life; I cared less for its appropriation by second-rate theoreticians. This woman had read, unbeknownst to me, a critical paper I had written, and now she wanted to discuss it, or rather, condemn me for not taking a more doctrinaire position. "I see why Walker likes you," she said dismissively, referring to the professor who had shown her my work. "You think like a man."

I had run into the woman at a faculty gathering, where everyone had had too much to drink and where the insults, liquor-whetted or not, tended to appear dressed up as compliments. Hers wore no such costume. She was saying, in as friendly a way as possible, that I was a traitor to my gender, daring as I had to embrace traditional critical or analytic discourse. I was dumbfounded by her accusation, and secretly a little pleased, though my reaction stops me now and makes me flinch at my uncertainties. If one believes synthesis and reason belong to a male domain, then I suppose she was right. But my pleasure came from someplace deeper and less articulable. I knew, because of the bent of my accuser, that I had leapt across the divide and landed. That I was writing tough, which was what I longed to do. The further I got in my life, the more I trusted my instincts; I had sworn I would never again genuflect before false or paltry idols. If that was what she called thinking like a man, then praise God and pass the ammunition. What I wanted, more than anything, was to think like myself.

Part Two

The past is never dead. It's not even past.

WILLIAM FAULKNER, *REQUIEM FOR A NUN*

Chapter Eight

My dad and I had a favorite story, traded back and forth over the years until it took on the comfort of an old flannel shirt. Neither of us could remember who told it first. It went like this: Once there was a mean old farmer who grew the sweetest watermelons in the valley. Partly because he was so ornery, boys from all over the county would sneak into his fields after dark to sample his crop. The farmer sat on his porch with a shotgun night after night, but he could never catch the boys in the act. One day after he'd had enough, he staked a big sign in the melon patch before dusk. It read: ONE OF THE WATERMELONS IN THIS HERE FIELD IS POISONED. Then the farmer went to bed and got a good night's sleep, certain that he had outfoxed the boys.

The next morning, he got up and went outside to look over his land. All the watermelons were intact. And alongside his warning sign, somebody had put up another. This one read: NOW TWO OF THE MELONS IN THIS HERE FIELD IS POISONED.

We loved this story. Whenever we told it, we would walk past each other for hours afterward and say, "Now *two* of the melons in this here field . . ." and start to laugh. My father liked it in part because he'd grown up on a farm where watermelons were a principal crop, and so he knew what it meant to harvest them, load them, guard them, and probably steal them. As the ninth of ten, he'd also had four older brothers to instruct him in the arts of being male; all of them, at some point or another, had been on at least one end of a gun.

It would be a good joke, of course, even if the melons were corn and the farmer was from Ohio. But there's something markedly Texan about the story, a distinction that has to do with its deadpan humor, its macho high jinks, its Old Testament payback. That old farmer got what he had coming, and nobody got hurt. It's a story about greed and effrontery, where wit trumps indignation and where the trickster-hero gets away in the end. The setup is a classic male coming-of-age tale, and you can find variations of it from Don Quixote to the Hardy Boys and Huck Finn. My father told me dozens of stories over the decades, repeated like litanies until we could each finish the sentences, most of them built on this scaffolding of conflict and triumph: Caldwell Agonistes, with laughs. In fact and fiction both, my father was an optimist. Despite the trials of a hardscrabble farm or a cold military base in northern England or a bigger, meaner kid on the playground, the lovable rogue—played, unerringly, by him—would always prevail.

But then stories have always been the hymns of history: From the grandest Homeric epic to a guy on the porch with his shotgun, they organize our dreads alongside our desires. For my father and me, the stories were how we talked—how he grasped and conveyed his past, the way he explained how he felt about the world, which he couldn't for his life have articulated without narrative props. In the bad years, the stories knocked down the walls between us, handing over morality tales and twists of fate without having to get too personal or accusatory. So there were stories about card games and scary fights and shows of strength or chivalry, most of them imparting a blend of courage, street smarts, and a little God-given justice. If I was lucky, he surrendered the point of the story and let the sweep of it take over, so that by the time I had left my own childhood, I had a profound visual impression of his: the boys he chased off the front porch from the farmhouse near Reilly Springs, the field where his brother Frank had been struck and killed by lightning. I knew relatives I would never meet in actuality, like Roy the prodigal son, and I knew all about the sweet, "slow" fellow named Walter whom my dad had befriended, five years older but in the same grade at school. "He just couldn't get out of the eighth grade," Bill would tell me. "We'd walk home together, and I'd say, 'Walter, how long are you gonna keep going to school?' Walter would smile and say, 'Just long enough to keep people from stealing my stuff.' "

After his dogged efforts to conquer fractions and the other hurdles of secondary school, Walter got a job as a short-order cook at a café in Reilly Springs; two decades later, he had saved enough money to buy out the owner. By any worthy measure, Walter's had been a triumphant life, and so this became our definition of true intelligence over the years: just smart enough to keep people from stealing your stuff. His invocation of Walter's life spoke to my father's assumptions about human nature and how to arm yourself against the worst of it. Crouching among the long rows of cotton fields in east Texas, separating fiber from boll, his older sisters had taught him the primary numbers when he was four or five; they used their raw knuckles as an abacus. Then his brothers had shown him how to fight—first with a paper sack (the poor man's punching bag) when he was little, and later, when he got old enough to use them, with a pair of boxing gloves. How to count and how to fight: He would claim these tutorials in self-defense as the most important of his life.

The stories, though, rarely acknowledged the humor that attended them, the poker-faced narrator who would never crack a smile. That, too, was part of the point: Never show your cards and never let on how funny you were, or even that there was any joke involved. This made the stories funnier, of course, because you couldn't see what was coming or how to respond, and the uncertainty kept you on edge, poised for drama or comedy either one. Thus it was that my sister especially loved the story about the branding iron, an affection compounded by the fact that, every time my father told it, my mother would roll her eyes and leave the room.

When he left Reilly Springs for college, my dad was six feet tall and weighed about 170 pounds. He was a wrestler and, from what I could later tell, was probably tough without being downright mean. He had a brattish younger cousin named Kenny who lacked the finesse of this distinction, and who, during a family reunion at the farm, had been goading my father and his brother Dick for days on end.

My father tolerated Kenny, who was probably thirteen or fourteen, until the kid stole his wallet and hid it somewhere as a prank. So Bill went out to the barn and got a branding iron, used for marking livestock, and buried it way down in the bottom of the freestanding deep freezer.

The next afternoon Kenny started in on his older cousins, delighting in the idea that, because they had yet to lose their tempers, they probably never would. Then my dad stood up from the table where he was playing cards, left the room for a minute, and walked back in carrying the branding iron, which had been in the freezer overnight and was smoking from the cold. By the time he'd crossed the room to Kenny and grabbed hold of his arm, the boy had fainted dead away.

My sister and I used to laugh so hard at this story that tears rolled down our cheeks, though the most dramatic expression we ever got out of my dad was a slow grin. "Kenny never did bother us again," he'd say, like he was surprised by the boy's falling for his ruse, though of course he wasn't, and he relished the effect of the story on his transfixed daughters. Long accustomed to her husband's narrative sway, my mother was rarely as amused or as credulous as we. She believed about half of what he said; the rest of the time, she would shake her head and say, unfailingly, "Why, that's the biggest bunch of bull I ever heard." For my father, who lived to get a rise out of my mom, her skepticism only raised the bar.

I wondered for years if these stories were true, until it dawned on me that it didn't matter, and it may have helped that we never

really knew. As with the useless antique Smith & Wesson revolver he kept by his bed, appearance was everything. The stories were true because the world they evoked was real—not just
the imagined one, but the atmospheric one, where a girl sat beside her father's chair thrilling to his mock-heroic tales, Sancho
Panza trying to hang on to her Don Quixote. Who cared if he was
tilting at windmills? The stories brought him home to me, told
me who he was, and then, because I listened, they encased me
like the sweetest fog. Like the watermelon tale, most of my dad's
were both dangerous and hilarious; in the hands of someone else,
the tales might assume pathological doses of machismo or ro-
manticized violence. But in his safekeeping, they were full of
drama, outrage, Faulknerian absurdity, the frisson of any great
narrative tension. No wonder I loved war novels. As I grew older,
the stories began to include things we had shared, and sometimes
the tale was so fine—so dressed up in words and gladness—that
it became bigger than the thing itself: It adorned the past and
then eclipsed it.

WHEN I WAS A GIRL OF NINE OR TEN, my dad would take me
along on autumn dawns to go quail and dove hunting, out to the
far reaches of the Caprock, past towns named Muleshoe and
Dimmitt to prairies so remote and unrelenting that even the
phone lines seemed to disappear as we drove into morning light.
I had hitched this ride into rough country as unofficial bird dog:
All I really had to learn, cloth bag in hand, was how to retrieve.

That I was going after quail, felled from the sky by his shotgun and still warm to the touch, didn't slow me down at all. Whatever myths we foster about a child's squeamishness are simply that; though I grew up surrounded by the tender fact of animals, by cats and dogs and even the cows and chicks on my grandparents' farm, I laid aside my affection when it came to watching my father hunt or fish. Instead I approached my duties with a child's gravity. Most of my mission—a timeless wait in an empty field—was as mesmerizing as it was undemanding. He was watching birds in flight, and I was watching him.

Because my father had grown up on the land, he knew how to make a living from it and would not abuse this hard education. He never killed anything he didn't eat, and he wouldn't hunt deer—he had tried it once, my mother said, and claimed thereafter he was too softhearted. If the winter was harsh, he placed feeders in the yard for birds and squirrels. But in autumn, at the start of dove or quail season, he would get out his fleece-lined hunting vest and the metal ammunition box he kept stored high on a shelf in the garage, along with the rags and oil he used to clean his shotgun. I remember these opening rites most intensely by smell: the old wood smoke on his vest from the previous year, the musk of the gun oil, the cold, sharp scent of early morning.

Why he took me along with him—well, certainly it was not to learn to shoot. I was still too young, and my father belonged to the Texas patriarchy that was overprotective of its females even as it drove them toward heroic feats. I think he just wanted the company—that, and he may have wanted to show me what was out there on those gorgeously bleak and empty plains. All that God and nothingness were the closest either of us ever got to a true sunrise congregation.

My father always contended that he'd lucked out by having daughters instead of sons. Boys were too mean, he told us, and he knew because he'd been one. So he gave to us the survival arts he believed in; like most men of his generation, he was far more comfortable enacting these skills than describing them. He taught me not just to go after the quail he'd shot, but how to clean and cook them, and he assumed these tasks with such poise that the act of hunting itself possessed for me a quiet dignity. I can see him silhouetted against that empty Texas plain, the birds overhead and a girl with a gunnysack nearby. Then he is standing in the alley behind our house, cleaning quail in the moonlight, his broad hands plucking and gutting the birds with calm expertise. The mingled smell of blood and birdshot and tobacco is the strongest memory of all—that, and the well-lit house that stood some twenty yards away, my mother calling from across the lawn.

And what did he gather up from those crystalline mornings, with the girl attendant to his every move? The father must look at the child and see within that small reflection all the fusion possible, all the anguish of separation that lies ahead. So this is how he stakes his claim, marks the heart of what is already his. Those graceful passages we shared would be his indemnity against the unknown territories of tomorrow. That is one of love's great laws: The father instructs, the child ingests, until memory itself becomes the long way home.

YEARS AFTER THESE DAY TRIPS were stored in the locks of adult consciousness, I found a snapshot of him taken by a hunting buddy at the end of a day shooting dove. The license plate on a Mustang in the background reads 1967, which means that my dad was in his early fifties in the picture, and I would have been sixteen. So our bird-dog days were far behind us by then, as was the taciturn camaraderie that defined those mornings. He is smiling at the camera, standing with a hand on his hip by the front of the car, where some two dozen dove lie spread across the hood. My surprise upon seeing this picture came not from the feathered quarry he is showing off, but from the resemblance, thirty-five years later, between hunter and daughter. He would have been the same age in the photo that I was when I saw it for the first time—a chronological shell game between the generations that we can witness only through images, whether canvas or celluloid or the scrawl on a cave wall. I gasped aloud at the picture, then asked a friend who was with me, a photographer, if he didn't think I looked just like my father. "Look like him?" he answered, smiling at what I couldn't see. "You even *stand* like him."

I WONDER WHAT SORT OF IDENTITY I was reaching toward, embedded there on the Panhandle plains. In the crevasses of childhood, the memories that carry the most resonance are those freed from the confines of gender: the card games and fishing trips, the insatiable requests for war stories from my laconic dad and then, when he wouldn't give, the return to the library's basement shelves. I painted my bedroom baby blue and I thrilled like every other girl over the emergence of breasts, but I was not exactly poised for Betty Crocker cook-offs in early Amarillo; my mother, whether distracted or subversive, mostly overlooked our training in the domestic arts. When I got to home economics in high school—all but mandatory in those days for a girl to graduate—I tore up my fingers learning to embroider, then accidentally set the cooking lab on fire. (This was not sheer ineptitude. I had been illicitly roasting marshmallows, and when the teacher walked in, I threw one, still flaming, in a drawer.) My sister had long since proved herself the athlete; besides my weak leg, I had a tendency to dawdle. But where Pam was a tomboy headed for glamour, I was a gangly girl who wore socks with loafers and couldn't figure out, despite her instruction, what to do with hair.

Introverts tend to be misunderstood in their families of origin, but in mine I was tolerated and even indulged—each of the four of us, riding the nuclear family's usual ship of fools, possessed idiosyncrasies that allowed for the others. My sister drew and sketched her horses, my mother fussed over her roses in the barren Texas soil, my father drove around town on Sundays at twenty miles an hour, his left arm hanging out the window. These were the activities not just of semi-small-town innocence, but of another age, when daydreaming was a necessary and legitimate activity. Having created his own small tribe, my father was alone in the company of females. It was clear he needed a sidekick, and I thought the job should fall to me.

However unwittingly, he became a co-conspirator in this game of chance. He taught me how to drive a stick shift, kick the tires, get on a horse, bait a hook, and reel in a hammerhead shark from an ocean pier, but in keeping with the system, he rarely asked what I thought about anything. He liked it when I stood up to him so long as it was a game of liar's poker: When we came back from fishing one day, after he'd spent the morning baiting my hook instead of his, he offered me five dollars to say that all the fish I'd caught belonged to him. The bribe was a fortune to a child—I must have been six or seven—and so I promptly agreed. Then we got within sight of the house, and I could contain myself no longer. I thrust the bill at him before running inside to report on my exploits. "Here's your five dollars," I told him solemnly. "I caught the fish."

The reason this story evoked so much paternal pride for all the years he told it had not a whit to do with integrity, but with the competitive nature he had glimpsed in me and then encouraged. My father was a relentless tease, but I always got the jokes, and it never occurred to me until decades later that some families actually had to make do without irony or pranks. He was a decent sport, too, in that he never backed down from his own instruction. When he was teaching me to drive, after I'd had enough of his overbearing advice, he got out of the car one day to trade seats with me, and I drove off and left him standing on the highway. I went only a few hundred yards, just far enough to unnerve him and then make him laugh, and this, too, became part of the collective mythology. I think he wanted more than anything for his girls not to be bamboozled, by crooks or life or maybe worst of all by men, and so every time either of his daughters showed a little muscle he privately applauded.

And yet for all the initiation rites and unspoken intimacy, the most crucial narratives that bound us were the ones we rarely mentioned. For two decades after I left home he meticulously polished my Lucchese boots every time I returned, but he refused to acknowledge that the feet those boots housed had never quite worked in tandem. "You mean that leg is still bothering you?" he asked me once, infuriating me, as though polio were something, like teenage rebellion, to be overcome or outlasted. No one in my life could make me angrier faster, but our recoveries could be just as swift, and the period of our long reconciliation was as sweet in its arc as the anger that preceded it had been thunderous. He told me twenty years after the last chopper had left Saigon that he thought I'd been right about the war in Vietnam, and he said this as casually as if we were talking about a passing rainstorm, and though I swallowed hard when he said it, by then I knew enough to leave it alone and treat it as the peace offering it was. I knew, too, that this was partly his way of saying *Thanks for growing up, finally, and for not getting in too much trouble, and now that you've shown some common sense, then OK, you can have your damn war, you can be right about this one thing.* The man was so stubborn and so proud of his own willpower that when he stopped smoking—a three-pack-a-day habit, Camels, for thirty years—he carried his cigarettes in his breast pocket for two months after he quit, just to prove that he could. It took me a decade to catch up with him, and during those years he pestered me to quit and offered me five hundred dollars to sweeten the deal. I stopped the day after I turned forty, and to my surprise I carried my pack around for a month after I knew I was through with them. I liked his bribe but would never let him make good on the bet, because, I told him, I wanted to have something, anything, on him. When he died the debt was still on the books, where it had been for years, which was the way we both wanted it.

HE COULD NEVER BEAR TO TALK MUCH about my heart. After I had lived two decades on my own as a single woman, he asked me out of the blue one day—I was forty-two—when I planned to get married and have children. We were alone, on our way to the airport, where I would board the inevitable plane back east. I looked at him in astonishment, poised for a fight, and then I saw the look of innocent regard on his face, and I burst out laughing instead. "You finally think I'm old enough, don't you?" I said, and he smiled, and said yes.

But then this was the way we had always talked, or not talked: Such father-daughter collusions of silence were commonplace for the men of his generation, who would no more break rank and lay bare their feelings than they would confess fear or self-doubt. In Texas, such fortitude found its counterpart in chivalry. When my father had taken his girls to the livestock exhibit at our first county fair—we were probably five and seven—we stumbled straightaway onto a pair of hogs mating in their pen. To a child, this was a fierce and wondrous thing: When the animals weigh six hundred pounds apiece, there is nothing like a full rut to make you see that love and war look remarkably alike. My sister asked with breathless glee what the hogs were doing; my father grabbed us both and began dragging us in the other direction. Playing, he said abruptly, and it was years before I could see behind his gruffness to the modesty it masked.

So I knew all about unspoken feelings and the rough, monosyllabic codes of love. I knew, or at least intuited, that anger could well be a mantle for tenderness and that courage was a trait best left unnamed. My familiarity with this stony strength in my own household was part of what drew me to Hemingway, or at least made me presume to understand his men. Like a lot of girls born of World War II vets, I had grown up with the code—in my house, it was pervasive as air. "Doesn't do to talk too much about all this," says the hunter in "The Short Happy Life of Francis Macomber," referring to the happy adrenaline rush of bravery. "Talk the whole thing away. No pleasure in anything if you mouth it up too much." So, too, with fear and its crueler legacies of fractured time and history: Nick Adams walking the country, "burned over and changed," and meticulously ordering his fragile life. I had seen my father go weak on me only once that I could recall, and it was when my mother was hospitalized for a couple of days for something minor. He was making dinner for the three

of us while she was gone—he was always at ease in the kitchen—
and my sister groaned when she found him cooking peas, which
all of us loathed. Why in the world did you make those things,
she asked, when none of us can stand them? "Your mother likes
them," he said softly, and spooned them onto all of our plates.

The peas brought her back to him, of course, confirming that
superstitious view of the universe that stress always elicits, and I
see now why this incident puzzled and scared me as a girl. My father's love for my mother was so great and so dependent that it
was essential as sunlight and almost as bright. When I wanted to
know how he felt about something serious—my grades, my
boyfriends, my arrest—I approached him like a wolf cub, wary
and wishful, but I only got within ten yards. If I wanted the long
version about anything, I asked my mother.

Or sneaked into the attic, where the trunk was kept, in which
she housed the letters he had written her from England. I could
disappear for hours upstairs without being bothered. So it was
there, camped on the crossbeams and insulation, that I first encountered the romantic who had courted my mother for two
years, then married her on a three-week leave. I found the snapshot from military training camp of a handsome fellow grinning
in a leather flight jacket, and the dog tags he had worn for three
years abroad—entwined, for luck, with a medallion bearing my
mother's maiden name. I found the wallet with his army pay-
card, his typhoid and smallpox inoculations, a tally-out list for
flame suppressors from his supply base in Blackpool, England.
There were folded copies of old Limey drinking songs and a

moth-eaten sergeant's cap and an adoring letter he had written my mother on their fourth day of marriage. What I had, in other words, was a cache of ordinary documents resplendent with history, and the man who starred in this ragtag drama was someone, inherently, whom the child can never know: the man your father was when you were at best a good idea.

The story that emerged from these letters was one I pieced together gradually, first with a daughter's curiosity and then within the arc of the war itself. He had shipped over to Blackpool as part of the Eighth Air Force in the spring of '43, just after his honeymoon, and stayed for the next three years. Because the Allied forces would not reveal the whereabouts of wartime troops, all his letters bore a nebulous dateline, scrawled at the top: "Somewhere in England" or "Same place in northern England." He wrote about shipments of watches and parachute silk, about getting his CO to arrange a visit from Joe Louis for his hangar, because his men were working overtime and couldn't stop to go see the heavyweight champ. Mostly, though, he wrote about how much he missed my mother. A letter from July 1944 began with a pitiful riff about having waited eight days for a letter from her:

> *You never have and I hope that you never do stand in a long line for two hours in a drizzling English cruel rain, twice daily for mail call—finally after what seems like a period of miserable years, you work your way up to the mail window to be told in a rough tone of voice—S/Sgt. Caldwell, you ain't got no **(*-(x**(mail today, you so-*

and-so. By then you have waited so long you can barely
stand, and make the mail man thumb through the C12
*just to be sure—to be told again that you have no **(xx.***
mail and quit taking up so much time. By then you are
more disappointed than a 6 mo-old baby that hasn't been
fed in 24 hrs. Your heart closes up in your throat—you feel
kinda dizzy and almost like crying—but you are too mad.
You turn around and you have to face some two hundred
guys all the way back the line who look at you—with a
murderous look in their eyes and a thought under their
breath of that S.O.A.B.—taking up so much time and he
didn't get a single letter.

Yes Ruby it is a cruel world and mail call without any
mail is about the worst Hell upon Earth—Just wanted
to take time to let you know how I feel when I don't hear
from you.

I CHERISH THIS LETTER not because it kindles any sympathy
but because it is my father at his high-drama best, full of bombast
and crocodile tears, and because I have the onionskin, ribbon-
wrapped proof that she wrote him nearly every day—*every day*—
for the three years he was gone. Because his birthday was June 3,
he wrote to her in the spring of 1945 that he believed it would all
be over soon, sometime near his birthday, and the censors held
this letter until after D-day on June 6 and then sent it on to her in
Texas. I have the magnificent letter she wrote him on May 8,

1945, in the final weeks of the German surrender; in Amarillo, on V-E Day, they closed the liquor stores and opened the churches. He would remain stationed in England for another eight months—America had the postwar job of getting millions of its soldiers home—and he was still prohibited from saying precisely where he was or when he would return. The letters from my mother during these last months are hopeful and then anguished and then chagrined by her lack of hope; she was reading the shipping news every morning, praying he would be on the next boat from Southampton. I found their letters wrenching in the yearning and poise they display, testament to what the two of them had been through and probably to the sort of life they would have together. Then came the Western Union telegram he sent on December 25, 1945, delivered to my mother in Amarillo at 11:34 p.m, from Camp Patrick Henry in Virginia: IM OVER HERE FROM OVER THERE AND WILL BE WITH YOU SOON LOVE.

Chapter Nine

FOR MOST OF HIS LIFE, my father would hardly talk about the war—not when I was a girl, and not much at all after I was grown, and my mother swore he never talked to her about it, either. Whenever anyone asked, he delivered the same concise narrative: He'd had it easy, he would say, safe in northern England; he'd never seen combat, and the worst casualties his men had suffered could be cured with a dose of penicillin—his euphemism for the gonorrhea that plagued the bases. Instead he talked around the war: about the fictional girlfriend he had invented to make my mother jealous (for years, we referred to her as Blackpool Mary), about the unending rain and the greasy fish-and-chips. And then finally, when he was past eighty and his leather armchair bore the permanent signature of his fondness for it, I asked him one night if he remembered D-day.

"Oh, yes," he said, and looked out the window, and I thought, *Now he's going to tell me something monumental.*

"You know, honey," he finally said, "I was a hell of a poker player in those days."

Because I had been listening to this kind of circumspect narrative all my life, I had the sense to keep my mouth shut and listen harder. I already knew some of the card-shark story: He had come back from England wearing a money belt with his poker winnings, which he swore to me amounted to nearly ten thousand dollars. I knew, too, that he was legendarily good at the game, so much so that he couldn't trust his own luck or ever take the low road and brag about it. "Once I drew four aces and a joker," he told me that night, with enough awe in his voice to make me think it was true. "And when it came time to lay down my hand, I only showed them the aces. I was afraid they'd kill me."

This was a classic Bill story: slyly self-effacing, dramatic, built around the idea that only you were getting the entire truth. That he had drawn four aces and a joker was a possibility with nearly incalculable odds; that he had waited fifty years to share the news was just as hard to believe. But these were my father's warm-ups; I had no doubt that the serious stories, if he told them at all, bore no such embroidery. The poker games, I hoped, would be the ante for the larger contest, the one that had kept him in England and that had changed the face of the modern world.

My patience paid off: My father told me more that evening about the Second World War than I believe he had told anyone, ever. He told me that the helmets of dead soldiers often wound up at his supply depot, where it was his unit's job to clean out the blood and sometimes brains and send them back to the front. He told me that he slept with a knife under his pillow for three years, and said the same prayer every night: *Dear Lord thank thee for letting me be alive today*. I found out, too, why he had opted to take a boat back to the States, even though it took him three weeks longer to get home: He had routinely watched the test pilots who flew in and out of his base, and one day had seen a pilot on fire hurl himself from a burning plane. He still wouldn't explain the scar near his rib cage that looked like a puncture wound, and I have a feeling he left out more than he told. This was a man who had spent a lifetime under the dictum of restraint, particularly when it came to bellyaching. "Don't tell people your troubles," he used to say. "Half of them don't care, and the other half think you had it coming."

The sweet incongruity of that *thee* in his nightly petition has always given me pause. It has the innocence of a child's prayer, like most foxhole devotions, and its quaintness is probably a leftover from my father's country-Methodist upbringing, where you thanked God for the good days and bought on credit during the bad ones. He was not an especially religious man—I think he assumed a divine presence, having neither the temperament nor the inclination to bear the alternative. But he began saying the prayer again in the last years of his life, at odd times and often more as incantation than plea, and only because he had told me about it that night, in reference to his years overseas, did I have any clue as to what it meant to him or where it came from.

WHAT NONE OF THESE STORIES or subtexts explains is my father's cussedness about the psychological consequences or aftermath of war. If he was dismissive about what he perceived as his own small role in the armed forces, he was wary and even intolerant when it came to stories of combat trauma—and yet even as I state this unequivocally, I realize I am wrong; it was only the unseen wounds of Vietnam he suspected as bluff. With the ruthlessness of selective hindsight, I have generalized his skepticism about Vietnam vets—about the vocal protesters who bore their pain as publicly as their medals—into something larger and less forgivable. The truth is that we may have never talked about the rest. When I invoked the bitter psychic casualties of Vietnam, the suicides and post-traumatic stress disorders and on-street despair, my father's response was unremittingly rough; for his money, these men were either faking it or had been lily-livered from the start. It was one of the worst differences between us, at least for me, and I can never know how reasoned his stance was, though I expect not very. I've learned enough from veterans over the years to know that other men's fear, laid bare, can make them crazy with anger or denial. I know that fear in combat can be dangerous as well as contagious: "Hysterical patients were left alone," wrote a battalion surgeon in his log account of medical operations at Belleau Wood in France, during some of the worst fighting of 1918. "This was the best treatment, and by so doing the valuable services of litter bearers were saved." If primitive instinct counsels us to shun the dead, war has taught us how to spurn the face of terror.

But men have always known. Since the first blood spilled on a bridge became a story, they've known, and the great folly is not their knowledge but their amnesia—every culture presumes to reinvent the myths. The myths are always connected and give birth to one another, Achilles paving the way for Verdun just as surely as a Southern boy dying on a Pennsylvania plain made somebody enlist a century later. That is the brilliant, sinister power of myth, which propagates as we sleep and dream away the chance for the story to turn out different: One war gives rise to the illusions of the next because we need the mythology to cover the mess. Otherwise we couldn't bear it; too much death and too many lousy, futile endings. It was my passion and ignorance to think that Vietnam invented mayhem, that any war was ever softer or worse than the rest, that young men had to face the murderer inside their own hearts before they died in the mud somewhere crying for their mothers. It was my duty, I thought, to believe this and to try to keep one more kid from giving it all up for McNamara, for Brown & Root, for imperialist hubris posing as nobility. But that was only the heart of a girl who had grown up on the old myths, where fathers go but come back safe, where at least you could use words like *sacrifice* and *hero* in the same sentence as *Normandy*. I had come of age, too, with *A Farewell to Arms* and *All Quiet on the Western Front,* so I ought to have remembered that no war had a corner on horror, just a better excuse for being there or a different way of procuring it, whether a trench or a catapult, though try telling a boy lying in the rain at Gettysburg without morphine that it would only get worse as history marched forward. Our fathers knew this, they all knew, as my dad did when he claimed that boys were mean and that human beings were capable of anything—and because they knew and had to keep going, they didn't talk much about it, and God knows they wouldn't talk about the fear. Writers and poets had been the ones to voice the irredeemable truths of war, even the death-sweet allure of it that held no higher meaning, and this, too, was a secret that shamed the men and so, like Hemingway's hunter, they left it alone.

MY DAD, HAD HE WALKED through such darkness or dared to dwell upon it, would have told me none of this—not just because he hadn't been on the front, but also because he was the kind of man who left the worst of life buried in the past. He had told me about knocking out a guy's teeth when he was in college—the man had insulted a woman they both knew, then came after my father with a broken whiskey bottle—but even his most brutal stories came out pretty tame in the end. He used a moral shorthand for the narratives with outcomes he couldn't affect, the tragedies where characters lost their moorings or had none to start. These tales were too sad, too real, and usually too close to the bone to be told straight out, so he wrapped them in caveats or warnings about what paths to avoid. The story of his brother Frank, killed by lightning in a field in Illinois, carried such severity, if only implicitly: He was sitting under a tree with his girlfriend during a thunderstorm, and he was so far from home when disaster struck that his body never made it back to Reilly Springs. But the preeminent character for this sort of apprehension was Roy—the first son of Della and Pink, a man whose splendid arc through life was rivaled only by his catastrophic end. He was nearly two decades older than my father, but had chosen Bill, the ninth of ten, as the sibling he would sponsor, sending his kid brother a hundred dollars a month to go to college during the Depression. Roy had died in the spring of 1941, only weeks before my parents met, and so the stories surrounding him took on another layer of fog-bound sorrow, open to vast interpretation.

Growing up with the lesson of Roy, all of it shrouded in sadness and enigma, somewhere I made the connection that to leave was to suffer—that such dazzling temptations as his came at great cost. Certainly he had assumed the role of a classic shooting star, beautiful and incendiary: the Columbia-educated lawyer, childless and far away, dead by his own hand at forty-two. The story and its projected possibilities hovered in the corners of my consciousness for decades, during my childhood and long after I had left Texas myself. But the real story, the more labyrinthine and astounding one, would not emerge until after all ten of the Caldwell siblings were gone.

Because my father had remained close to Roy's widow for the rest of her life, she had named him the executor of her estate. Helen had died in 1996, and the few papers left from her affairs were filed in my father's office. I found them by accident, the week after he died, when I was helping my mother search for his birth certificate. There amid old family documents and photographs was a battered accordion file containing the remnants of Helen's life. In the years it had been there, I doubt anyone had given it more than a cursory look.

I'd seen photos of Roy before, of course, but mostly they were shots taken in Reilly Springs, on one of his rare trips back to Texas. Here was the evidence of that broader life I had heard so much about, of New York and Europe in the 1920s and '30s. There were pictures of the golden boy in Spain and in lower Manhattan, letters bearing his address as 19 Christopher Street in the West Village, which did little to diminish the romance. A notice about the opening of his law practice in 1932, at One Broadway in Manhattan. And a torn clipping from a Dallas newspaper in 1921, announcing that Roy had been awarded the Carnegie Peace Foundation Fellowship in international law; he was the first Southerner ever to receive it. Immersed as I was in the mundane details of early grief, I was scanning this story, half-distracted, until I glanced down at the last paragraph and saw the words *Soissons front,* and something cold opened up inside me. I did the math and was aghast I had not done it before. "Mother," I said carefully, "was Roy in the First World War?"

"Why, yes," she said, with a calm I had heard her use before to deliver profundities. "He was in France, for two years. He was *gassed.* You mean Bill didn't ever tell you?"

Here was what I read that day, or rather, the beginning of what I would read:

Mr. Caldwell was one of the 21 cousins who rallied to the flag, at Uncle Sam's first call for volunteers. He served two years in the Medical Department of Ammunition Trains going through the terrible days on the Soissons front, on down to Chateau-Thierry, and through the Marne Pocket, being gassed at Fismes. Was also in the Argonne Forest Campaign. Was in the Army of Occupation at Coblenz.

So this, too, was who my uncle Roy had been—a man who had left college to enlist at eighteen, gone to France, seen firsthand all the grim and deadly horrors I had spent half my life reading about. I knew enough by now to interpret what I was seeing here and to have an idea of the enormity of what he had endured. This would mean he had gone overseas with the first wave of the American forces—"Retreat?" they would say, legendarily. "Hell, we just got here!"—that picked up the ruins of the devastated French and English armies and helped force the German surrender. This would mean he had lived through the cruel stasis of so many dead on the front in France and no ground gained, in those summer months of 1918. He had been in some of the worst fighting of the American Expeditionary Force, when to live through an hour in a trench at Fismes could be bad enough to leave a part of you there forever. I had before me his Soldier's Individual Pay Record book, his enlistment record, his honorable discharge. I had the vital statistics—"18 10/12 years of age, student, 5 feet 7½ inches in height, single, character excellent"—and the list of battles, engagements, expeditions: "Alsace Sector 6/12 to July 21—1918. Aisne, Marne off July 29 to 8/7/18. Oise-Aisne off 8/26 to 9/6/18. Meuse-Argonne." I had it all, in faded ink on crumpled paper, redolent with the scents of age and life and death. "Finally only the names of places had dignity," Hemingway had written about this war, and here, in my father's office, were some of the names.

STANDING THERE AT THE DESK, dulled with the slow intensity of the newly bereaved, I was staggered by what I was holding—by what it had taken for me to find it, and to understand what I was seeing. This was the unarchived story of Roy H. Caldwell, private first class, Artillery Unassigned, "L.O. Med. Det 107th Am. Tr.," that I was never going to see or hear about anywhere else. Here was a view more dispassionate, maybe more honest, than memory will ever be, and it had fallen to me, a niece unborn when Roy died, but someone whose heart still seized at the words *terrible days on the Soissons front.* My mother told me that day that Roy's lungs were permanently injured from the gas he'd taken at Fismes; that he came home ill and frail in 1919 and never recovered, despite the images he had cultivated of a high-flying life in New York. The clipping describing the 1921 Carnegie Peace Foundation Fellowship, for research he would do on the arbitration codes of The Hague, took on another level of meaning. Among Helen's papers was the memorial book from his funeral two decades later in Manhattan, overflowing with tributes and signed by more than a hundred people; forty of them, including a police chief and a prince and princess, had sent flowers. The last names in the book were those of my father and his older brother Dick, who had gone to New York to claim Roy's body. Then I found the yellowed front page of the *Daily Times Herald,* the Dallas newspaper of record dated April 3, 1941, with a story bearing the headline FORMER TEXAN DIES IN GAS-FILLED ROOM OF APARTMENT HOUSE. It was a wire report of a few sentences, and they got his age wrong by five years:

New York, April 3 (INS).—Roy H. Caldwell, 47-year-old lawyer formerly of Commerce, Tex., was found dead Wednesday in his apartment kitchenette where gas poured from four open jets on a stove. A note was found addressed to his wife, Mrs. Helen M. Caldwell in Daytona Beach, Fla. Police said the attorney had been despondent because of poor health.

But it was not a note. It was a letter scrawled across seven pages, and I found that, too.

Tuesday

Helen, darling:

This is a very difficult note or letter to write to you. Dearest, I have reached My end—financially and physically—and can't carry-on. I want to tell you that I have and do love you more than all other things.

I must go and as I am [illegible] *today and give you an opportunity to secure some joy in life. . . .*

[A long accounting follows of existing assets, life insurance policies, and outstanding debts, the substance of which led my father to believe that Roy died penniless. Also his instructions to Helen, who had gone fishing with her father, about his law firm, Gazan & Caldwell, which he believed owed him money.]

Darling, I have and do love you above all things, and while you have been a beautiful wife I have not been the husband I wanted to be—my nerves have been gone for years—and I am very sick now—forgive me!

Write nothing to my family as my passing will mean little.

Darling, I trust that I go quickly today—and my last thoughts are of you.

Farewell, darling.

R.

ASSAULTED OR LIFTED UP BY LIGHT, memory will always travel where it needs to go. I can never know what kind of stamp his brother's life and death made on my father, or if the hard fact of Roy's wounds from the front in 1918 shaped how my father would feel about other men hurt by other wars. I do know that my dad needed to believe that poverty and debt were what had killed his oldest brother. These would have constituted endurable losses: troubles he understood, did not judge, and knew he could conquer if he saw them coming down the road. And maybe I need to believe the other truth, the other destroyer named in Roy's letter—"my nerves have been gone for years"— because that is a battle whose coordinates I can locate; that is a sacrifice I know is heroic and a loss I can comprehend.

I know, too, this one thing. That however gifted or courageous Roy was throughout his life, he was wrong about something vital in those final hours before he turned on the jets. He must have long been in that narrow corridor of the suicidal, where the walls grow ever higher and the idea of death itself, of what it will do to the living, begins to seem inconsequential. Suicides have to believe this, usually a great lie, in order to find the momentum to go. It is a place void of much emotion, I think, and as desolate as any gray dawn over no-man's-land. But whatever else he clung to or discarded that last spring day, Roy was mistaken when he told Helen not to write his family, "as my passing will mean little." I was still a decade away from being born, but it would not mean little to me.

MAYBE IT BELONGS TO EVERY GENERATION to mourn the mistakes and bodies of the past. The witnessing is what verifies the loss; Edith Piaf singing "La Vie en Rose" would not be so wrenching outside the context of Vichy France. Staring at the long, urgent script of Roy's last words to Helen, I can hear the radio in the next room announcing that more troops are going to Iraq; the ones already there cannot come home, a faux conscription the military calls Stop Loss. So yes, the myths are always connected, Odysseus resisting the call of the Sirens only because the dead warned him of their power. The myths we know about are always less dangerous than the ones we don't; Freud was right about that. The strongest hidden narratives act as divining rods, ordering your life path without even bothering to show you the map. And tonight, while I'm wishing Edith Piaf were piped into every household in America, somewhere a boy stands up in his bedroom, decorated with rock posters and a trophy or two, and decides to go over there and help out.

I WALK THESE DAYS IN A NEARBY CEMETERY, centuries old, with acres of faded marble and exquisite tributes to the dead. Patrician New England names are buried here, Peirce and Brattle and Whitworth, their commemorative slabs bearing noble recitations of history itself. The smaller stones tell different, softer stories: names known only to their survivors, who leave flowers and sometimes photographs and the aching signatures of life's forward march.

The veterans' field is a simple and elegant sprawl of flat stones arranged alongside the main road that abuts the cemetery. Originally this part was laid out chronologically, beginning with the graves of men from the Civil War and the Spanish-American War. Then the world wars brought too many additions to the field, and so the rows reversed and began again. Small white markers on the trees direct you from one war to the next: WWI, WWII, KOREA AND VIETNAM.

This month, in autumn, the plots in the newer part of the veterans' field are adorned with Red Sox pennants—the home team has just won the World Series for the first time since 1918, and so the celebration extends here, too, its billowing flags placed upon dozens of graves. An early storm has shrouded the cemetery in a few inches of snow, and the drifts have settled away from the flat stone markers to the ground around them, so that the field has an eerie look of perfect symmetry—as though some thoughtful God had herded the falling snow away from the stones, then framed them with modest rises of white.

I have never before noticed this phenomenon, which is surely a consequence of temperature bumping into mass: The sun must warm the stone ahead of the grass. The field is not yet full; there will always be room for boys coming home in flag-draped caskets, to lie next to and then beyond the plots reserved for Korea and Vietnam. But today I have something to tell them all. Johnny Damon led off with a home run in the fourth pitch of the game, I want to say, and from that moment on, it was a triumph waiting to happen. Today, with all these pennants rippling across their graves, I salute the entire field.

* * *

MY FATHER GAVE ME GREAT GIFTS—courage and determination and card skills and the rest—and also burdens: anger, willfullness, an inability to know when to quit. This last trait could manifest as pitiable or dangerous, depending on circumstance. When I was about sixteen he was offered a good deal on an old '63 Ford Falcon and decided it was the right car for his girls, so he made me go with him out to the little town of Panhandle, thirty miles east of Amarillo, to make the deal and then drive home in tandem. Within two minutes behind the wheel, it was evident why my dad had gotten such a bargain: A standard, three-speed on the column, the car wouldn't go faster than thirty miles an hour. I was driving this junker; he was next to me in his spotless Ford sedan, and of course he blamed me for our sorry state of affairs. He shook his head, exasperated; he rolled his eyes at what had to be my bad driving; he motioned for me to pull over. We stopped both cars beside the highway and switched vehicles, to my relief and delight; now it was my turn to watch. Then he eased the miserable little Falcon into traffic, puttering along at the same torturous crawl. But my father refused to give in. He drove next to me, grinning and waving, all the way home, as proud as a horseman on a champion steed. He would not, could not, concede defeat, even when to stand firm made him look like a fool. Admitting that the Falcon was in fact a turkey would be to acknowledge that he had been taken. Two days later, to my mother's amused disbelief, he sold the car for a slight profit; I allowed him a few weeks of prideful silence before razzing him about the deal.

So if Marx was right that history repeats itself first as tragedy, next as farce, it was my good fortune to take some of my father's lessons on the chin. By the time I left home I was as bullheaded and sometimes as belligerent as he, though sixty pounds lighter and without the sense yet to distinguish between courage and bluff. I was a carnivore who hated war, a feminist who thought it her autonomous duty to be able to use a gun. These were hardly contradictions in the early 1970s—it was the heyday of the back-to-the-land movement—and I spent several desultory months testing their parameters when I lived on a farm thirty miles southeast of Austin, on a bend of the Colorado River.

The nearest town was Bastrop, ten miles away, where one went for groceries and for some of the finest barbecue in the region, served up in the back of the local meat company on Main Street. To get to the brisket counter, lined with pickles and saltines and towering stacks of white bread and napkins, you first had to cross through the butcher shop, where huge sides of beef hung alongside the carving tables. The people who made it past this brutish entrance hall were serious folk; the wooden tables at the back of the shop, where you sat down to eat, had steak knives chained underneath the boards every couple of feet. Between shifts of diners, a woman would come by with a bucket of soapy water, dip the knives, then wipe them off with a rinse rag. The place had been there since the 1930s, and the knives looked nearly as old; I assumed they were bolted down so that people wouldn't steal them. Eventually the locals told me another story: that the practice had gone into effect after too many rough Saturday nights when unruly customers had tried to use the knives on each other instead of the meat.

Over in Utley, where the farm was, we could hardly match such carnivores' aggression, but we did have an idealized fantasy of unblinking self-sufficiency. We kept chickens on the farm, along with a dozen or so rabbits, though none of the rotating crew of humans who lived there could bear to kill any of them for food. Instead we pretended; we feigned a version of agrarian autonomy, with our pickup trucks and giant cornstalks and melon patches, but we scurried into Austin for movies during heat waves. I did, however, like to fish, and one evening I was standing outside the house, trying to clean and gut a carp I had caught that day in the Colorado.

The fish was huge, almost two feet long, and I was halfway through the battle when I knew I didn't have it in me. It didn't help matters that I was stoned, a state that heightened the murderous fact of my enterprise but hardly enhanced my skill. I got the belly emptied and the head partly off, and then I looked up to see the sky going from dusky blue to black, and I knew that whatever I thought I was doing out here, it was a long cry and a thousand miles from the Caprock at dawn with my dad. For a minute, staring at a fish that was staring back at me, I felt like I was losing my mind; I closed my eyes and stood there holding on to the worktable. I didn't want to be good at killing what I ate—I didn't know what I wanted, from life or even from my next meal, but I knew with the certainty of pot-laced epiphany that this wasn't it. I said some nonsense, pantheistic blessing over the carp, then wrapped it in three layers of foil and threw it in the back of an old freezer on the porch. It stayed there for more than a year, because I couldn't bear to admit that I had killed something badly and for no good reason.

Fabricated warrior rites aside, these are hurdles, at least symbolically, that every young person has to face or clear; they have to do with independence and self-regard and the way you learn to navigate the world. But I had raised the bar by politicizing such pursuits and by assuming I had to handle everything alone. I'd already been tested that same week when a seven-foot-long chicken snake, harmless to humans and native to south Texas, had gotten into the empty henhouse, next to the rabbit cages. The chickens were in the yard and started making a ruckus, and when I realized the cause of their distress, I went tearing out there, insanely, with a .25 automatic pistol. A broom and a loud voice would have been far better choices as weapons. But I was trying to prove something, I think—that I could defend what I loved, that I knew how to handle trouble—and so I fired at the snake, sending it slithering back into the brush and traumatizing the rabbits for probably the rest of their lives. Then I stood there shaking with adrenaline, chagrined by my own absurdity, and I had one of my first adult glimmerings that most of the battles in life were not going to be so straightforward. That they would require, as Stephen Dedalus said, silence, exile, and cunning, not an arsenal of firepower or a show of force. Otherwise you have a standoff you never wanted—between man and beast, army and army, father and daughter. Otherwise what you have is a tin hutch full of freaked-out bunnies who never actually needed your aid; you have a Saturday-night special and a nonpoisonous reptile thinking, were he to think at all, that you just wasted a whole lot of nothing on the wrong guy.

IN HIS LAST YEARS, the arthritis my father had first contracted in England gradually overcame him until he couldn't get around, or even stand, without the aid of a walker. He did not surrender to the fact of this infirmity until long past when he should have, after several months of precarious pitches and dives, and then only when my mother's best friend dropped off a walker, festooned with ribbons, on the front porch. After that he was never without it, even to cross the room.

But he insisted on attending a weekly men's club luncheon every Tuesday, and during one of my trips to Amarillo I drove him to the place. He got out of the backseat, walker in tow, and began the long ascent up the handicapped-access ramp—about ten yards from the car to the door, where an attendant stood waiting. My dad declined any help, and I refused to leave, so I sat in the car with my mother next to me until he got inside.

It took him five minutes. He would move the walker forward a few inches, pull his feet up after it, then stop and rest, his arms leaning on the walker as though he were surveying the scenery. Every couple of steps, he looked back at me, smiled and waved. Then he would begin again. When he got inside, I turned to my mother with tears on my face. Hers was a placid sea; she was used to this sort of behavior from him. "Good God," I said. "And to think I ever wonder how I got so stubborn."

"BLOOD, I SAYS, governors and generals," says Jason Compson, Quentin's older brother in *The Sound and the Fury*. "It's a damn good thing we never had any kings and presidents; we'd all be down there at Jackson chasing butterflies." That's a bull's-eye grasp of madness and power if ever I heard one, and Faulkner left it to his most irascible character to deliver the link with such tough precision. My immediate family had escaped the doom-infested territories of classic tragedy, but all families endure, like Faulkner's noble Dilsey, in response to the past, whether in concert or in sharp discord. Both the Caldwells and the Groveses had known their share of midcentury strife, and each of my parents had fled Reilly Springs and Breckenridge as resolutely as I would turn my back on Texas a half century later. I don't believe there was a pillar of salt for any of us on that flat horizon. After a while, mobility itself becomes a kind of poetry—with hope and distance working in sweet cahoots, and momentum being the meter that carries you along.

Chapter Ten

IN 1951, THE YEAR I WAS BORN, America was at the height of a polio epidemic that had been playing out for most of the twentieth century. The Salk vaccine would not be proved effective until 1955, and public fear about the disease was manifest in the daily papers, which published a running tally of new cases during summer months, when the virus struck the hardest. Photographs of Franklin Roosevelt in his wheelchair, his legs covered with a blanket of stoicism, had made polio part of the common vocabulary and probably granted its victims a modicum of dignity, but the other images, the ones from the heightened outbreaks after the Second World War, were sadder and scarier: March of Dimes poster kids wrapped around their metal crutches, quarantine signs posted outside the closed public swimming pools. Worst of all was the medieval creepiness, in name and appearance, of the iron lung, a huge apparatus that helped victims breathe when the virus hit their respiratory tract. Partly because of the wholesale triumph of the Salk and Sabin vaccines, the disease and its aftermath seemed both mysterious and commonplace. It blew through the general population with the nonchalant force of a hurricane, and then was gone—its casualties, limping or wheelchair-bound, the only proof it had ever existed.

Popular culture usually holds the clues to society's worst fears, and the circuses and county fairs crisscrossing America in the 1950s were a back-alley testament to this. Amarillo lay on the road-show circuit along Route 66, and so my sister and I lived for the summer fair, especially its creepier aspects. Once we'd had enough of the cotton candy and the Tilt-a-Whirl, she and I would sneak away to the forbidden lane known as the freak show, a badly lit row of exhibits on the edge of the fairgrounds. Most summer carnivals had this little suburb of the bizarre, where you could gaze upon such pseudohorrors as the Snake Man, the Bearded Lady, the baby in a jar, and the boy in an iron lung. It now seems preposterously macabre, even by traveling-fair standards, that a critical polio victim would be on display alongside Tarantula Girl or the Fattest Man in the World; maybe the boy was in truth the carny barker's healthy son. But I still remember him lying there in a huge metal tube, fighting for his every breath. And I remember the hideous rhythm of the iron lung, a relentless sound of punctuated gasps.

Most polio victims were far luckier than the exhibit boy, if indeed his distress was real; some of us never even knew we'd had it. A virus that attacked the nervous system, poliomyelitis had probably been endemic for centuries, until advances in public health had lessened the infection rate in infancy, when cases were milder and its victims would gain resistance. By the 1940s and '50s, in the last years before the vaccine, the disease reached its apex; the summer of 1952 alone saw sixty thousand new cases.

Those were the ones severe enough to be noted and reported, when parents might see their child go to sleep with a fever or headache, then wake a few hours later unable to move. Innumerable milder cases, misdiagnosed or dismissed as flu, left no trace except for blessed immunity. I was six months old when I contracted polio, too young to verbalize any complaint or to display muscular weakness, and so the doctors assumed that my raging fever, which lasted about two weeks, was an inconsequential virus that would run its course. Then I didn't walk. I would stagger to my feet, fall, and try again, but I was two and a half before I took my first steps; when I did, I threw my right leg out at a desultory angle, relying on the stronger left one to even me out.

Young as I was, I still have traces of recall about this early futility: I remember the color and feel of the living room carpet, which must have risen up to meet me far too many times, and I still associate it with defeat. All my life I've had dreams of crawling, exhausting but Sisyphean, because I never stop. What my debility meant developmentally, I have to surmise from the theorists. Determined like any child to rise—to do what the body and mind are engineered to do—I met with an inordinate amount of failure; this went on, my mother tells me, for eighteen months instead of the usual few. But physical frustration could not thwart the mind's imperative: I suspect that, as with anyone bound by external circumstance, I threw my focus inward and began to travel there.

Amazing to me now, I didn't give up, a tenacity I attribute mostly to my mother, who began working in earnest to strengthen my leg. Our job entailed a regimen of exercises, done every morning for a couple of years when I was four and five. She would lie next to me on the floor, our legs propped against the wall, and begin toe-walking up and down its surface while I followed in tired imitation. We did leg lifts and heel stretches for an hour or longer each day, an eternity for a child, until I couldn't tolerate any more. But my mother's equanimity encouraged mine. Because she never displayed frustration or dismay, she saved my spirit while she rebuilt my leg. I had a few grim areas of girlhood yet to conquer—I could never ride a bicycle, and for a few years I was ordered to wear horrid corrective saddle oxfords, which I stashed in my school locker in exchange for a pair of girlish flats. Mostly, though, I learned to navigate the world slightly off-kilter, a position that reflected how I felt inside and that eventually seemed insignificant. By the time I reached adolescence, I could fake my way through the six-hundred-yard run, and I saved face in gym by becoming the class clown. In those pre–Title IX days, when being cool was considered superior to athletic prowess, I'd managed to turn my limp into a saunter.

In the decades they've had to study the long-term physical and psychological effects of polio, medical historians have found that its victims tend to be driven people who diminish the impact of the disease on their lives or deny it altogether—a description I find humbling in its familiarity. Yet I feel sure that, as with many minor infirmities, mine merely slanted the life rather than defining it. If polio cinched the deal that I would never be a track star, it may instead have made me a swimmer; water was the one place where I didn't feel off-balance. Almost certainly it ensured that I would be a reader. Unable to navigate the territory around me, I must have sent this stream of desire underground, assuring or at least accentuating an introspective personality.

And there is my mother, patient and present, helping me toe-walk up those monochromatic walls. The worst moment in this archive of weariness comes from when I was about four. The orthopedist treating me was a cold, overbearing man whom I still recall with loathing; he should have been given a sawhorse instead of a stethoscope. He insisted during one visit that my mother put me in a leg brace while I slept, and when we tried it that night, I woke up screaming from the pain. The brace was designed to stretch and thus lengthen the underdeveloped muscles of the lower leg. My memory of the night is vivid but not awful, because I can still see the slant of light outside my bedroom door; I can hear my mother running toward me down the hall. I remember being saved, in other words, and so the rescue has eclipsed the torment. She tore the thing off me, and we never went near it again.

I know now that the disease left a relatively faint mark on our door. Unaware in those first few years that I had even contracted the virus, my parents must have gone from initial dismay to relief and then joy that I was walking at all. If polio had taken something, we didn't know what or how much, and so their innocence probably protected us from useless fear. My father, choosing his familiar route of forward march, all but refused to believe I was ever hindered, in any way, from anything. My mother was operating intuitively, both when she pressed through those years of leg exercises and when she refused to inflict pain on her child, and her instincts turned out to be more effective than any diagnostic tool. But she was also giving me something less conscious or apparent, and that was a certain headstrong courage—a determination and emotional autonomy that thrived on solitude. For a girl with a weak leg and a penchant for the inner life, few resources could have mattered more.

Most of the cornerstone truths in families are unstated, and one of ours was my mother's self-contained strength—no woman could have survived the headwinds of my father's personality without her own angle of repose. She could lose herself for hours in her garden, at her sewing machine, and in the novels she consumed, and I took her serene focus as the blueprint for a life. When my father had to travel on business, usually for a night or two every few weeks, he complained about being away from us. My mother never disdained this affection, and yet I remember our evenings without him as tacit conspiracies of pleasure: She didn't have to cook, and we three got to be left alone to read. My sister and I would pile in the back of the old Ford station wagon, and we would all head for the Dairy Queen, where each of us sat in blissful silence, a book in her lap, eating cheeseburgers and fries and turning pages. If this charbroiled reverie seemed to me the ultimate contentment, I also recognized it as a private delight—I thought it would hurt my dad if he'd known how happy we'd been, slouched against the car seats, ordering malts and reading in the summer twilight until darkness sent us home. Decades would pass before my mother told me how she had stolen away from her brother and sisters to read when she was a girl, sitting with her book while she ignored their cries of play as they searched for her. She relayed this story half apologetically, as though she shouldn't have needed the retreat, should have been a more involved oldest sister. But what she perceived as coolness or disregard, I construed as freedom—I saw her crime of passion as an act of liberation.

In such ways feminists, maybe writers, are born: Emulating my mother as any child will, I grew up feeling the dreamy luxury of staring out the window, of lying in the backyard counting Johnny-jump-ups (I got to five hundred before I gave up), of writing bad lines of poetry that I knew nobody but my mother would read. These were headwaters, rather than ambitions; they were states of mind. My mother was our version of Mrs. Ramsay: the oak tree in the corner of the canvas, fixed and essential. She created the tableau, then made room for us to live within it.

My most exotic memory of my mother from when I was a child belongs to an evening she was going out on the town with my dad. Given the paucity of Amarillo's nightlife, I cannot imagine where they would have gone—they were not the type for the cowboy bars or the symphony, and the city didn't offer much in between. Maybe a road show or traveling orchestra had come to town. But what I remember was the black-and-gold lamé dress she was wearing, the swoony power of her perfume, and the way she hugged me when she left. When she came home late that night, after the babysitter had gone, my sister and I convinced her to do a few steps of the jitterbug, which she performed with joyful precision. And no child of the most glamorous sophisticate ever felt more richly blessed.

As we need them less but know them better, our images of parents shift over time—if we are lucky, we trade in dependence or anger or idealization for the long view of compassion. My mother changes in my mind's eye through the decades from the brunette bombshell she was when she married my father to the reservoir of dignity she grew into as she aged, though these are the refracted images of memory, the interior album pages that every consciousness catalogs and hoards. And they are memories independent of me: When I scan the portrait for its legacies, she emerges less as fierce mother bear than as levelheaded liberator.

The life passages that could have proved injurious did not: We survived the mother-daughter anguish of adolescence with a mutual regard that helped us even in the worst times. She had suffered my estrangement with forbearance, whether trying to rescue me from Travis or from a Lubbock jail; when Pam, my sister, advised her to leave me alone, she even tried that, though it must have been the hardest act of all. During the height of the antiwar movement, when I had dropped out of college and was hitchhiking around the country with all the gravitational force of a ball bearing, my mother, sick with worry, consulted an elderly family physician in Amarillo who hadn't laid eyes on me since I was a child. I was living in Austin and hadn't been near Amarillo in some time. But the doctor heard my mother say the words *antiwar protests* and *hitchhiking* and, like any red-blooded fool in those days, promptly announced that I was in trouble and that he thought I might need shock treatments.

This zealous long-distance diagnosis now strikes me as both comic and horrid. Like the orthopedist flummoxed by my noncompliant leg, the man wanted to wrestle into submission what he could not mend. But he must have terrified my mother, whose own sister had undergone shock treatments for terrible depression a decade earlier. Still, she had the sense to ignore the doctor's grim speculation. Instead she got in her car, put one of my dad's hats in the back window to camouflage the fact, she was traveling alone, and drove the five hundred miles to Austin. She located my address on a city map and knocked unannounced on the front door. There were four dogs and roughly five unrelated humans living in an old house in west Austin, and we welcomed my mother with the sort of brown-rice hospitality you would expect in those days. Gracious and tight-lipped, she declined our offer to sleep on the floor and took a hotel room nearby; she stayed for three days and spent most of them talking to me. Because she had the nerve and good sense to come looking for her daughter on her own, she found me.

Like the man she married, my mother did not suffer fools, but she didn't brag much about the trait, either. When I left Texas for the Northeast, she alone knew the precarious nature of my actions: knew that I had no job and no place to live, only a great desire to go. She told me to go and she softened the truth for my father, sending me a check to buy a decent coat that first miserable winter, when I was living on nothing but noodles and cheap

Scotch and fear. And she wrote me dozens of letters, long, eloquent letters typed on her IBM Selectric, recently upgraded from the old Royal manual that had been as central to her life as an anvil is to a blacksmith. Silent and subversive, she had long before lit a lamp on a darkened landscape, then said not a word as I walked toward its glow.

THE FARM NEAR BRECKENRIDGE, Texas, where my grandparents lived was a ten-acre scrub patch covered with mesquite, hackberry, and pecans, thirty miles west of a lake called Possum Kingdom. You can tell by looking at mesquite that it thrives in heat. Gnarly and tough, the trees are all over central Texas, where an average July afternoon can reach ninety-eight degrees. Toward the end of the long drive there in summers, my heart used to sink when I saw the mesquite—wave after wave of it, spread like some enemy camp we had to pass through to get to the farm. A little town of about six thousand by then, Breckenridge had been a boomtown for oil in the 1920s, and my granddad Jerome had worked as an oil pumper for years, maintaining the huge Bessemer engines they used to run the rigs. He and my grandmother Letha Iva lived in the oil camps with their growing family for about five dollars a month. Like most men who worked the rigs—the drillers and wildcatters and roustabouts—Granddad saw none of the profits of the boom and too large a share of the work. After the gushers were spent and Breckenridge settled down again, he and Mamaw did the only thing they could in that kind of heat: They put their life savings into a place big enough for a few hundred chickens, then spent the rest of their lives trying to make those birds happy.

Besides the rambling old house near the highway, with a couple of porches built onto either end for the breeze, the farm had three or four henhouses, a front office where the incubator was kept, a barn, a fruit cellar, and a tank for the cows. Heading down the road toward the farm, you could see the pink neon sign—FRESH EGGS—that my granddad had hung in front of the house in the 1950s. People came from all over the area for the eggs, which Mamaw wrapped neatly in a paper sack and sold for about fifteen cents a dozen. As soon as she heard a car coming down the gravel driveway, toward the back of the house, she would head outdoors to meet them. Because he was a man who could sell water to a fish, my dad loved this job, and during our visits he would try to wrestle it away from Mamaw; he usually got her an extra nickel for the eggs.

Perhaps only to a child can a place seem simultaneously thrilling and boring, which is how I remember the farm. My grandparents had bought the place after my mother had left home, but as a girl I could not make that distinction, so I viewed it simply as the repository of my mother's youth. It was a world I associated with languid summer vacations, rowdy cousins, tapestries of country stars, and the smells of my grandmother's cooking—platters of fried chicken, huge, sweating pitchers of iced tea, cast-iron pots of pinto beans baked all day in the oven with brown sugar and salt pork. The only thing that rivaled these feasts was the announcement that preceded them: When she had the meal ready on the outside tables, Mamaw would go up on the cement stoop, cup her hands around her mouth, and holler "DinnEERRRRRRRR!!!!!" with all the melodious expertise of a hog farmer or an auctioneer. She sang and played the organ in the local Baptist church, and she had a strong alto that hit operatic possibility on that second syllable, and the kids—our mouths already watering—would start running toward her cry.

She was always cooking: fried eggs for my granddad, coconut or custard pies, skillets of corn bread for the pinto beans. I don't remember my grandmother ever resting until the last decade of her life, when she finally sat in a rocker on the back porch, her old blue jeans rolled up to her knees, shelling fresh black-eyed peas or just rocking. Until then she had either been at the stove or tending to her chickens, two or three hundred of them, kept in aluminum henhouses lined with laying racks and water troughs. She was out there by dawn every morning and several times during the hot summer days, and sometimes, when I was small, she would take me with her to feed the chickens—I would hold on to her pants leg at the knee while she scattered feed from the bucket she carried. "Chiiiicccckk! Chick chick chick!" she would call, and the birds would go crazy trying to get to her, careering off their perches or running toward us along the dirt floor. Chickens can't fly very far or high; they fling themselves through the air and parasail for a few yards before using their claws as brakes. Because I was no taller than Mamaw's waist—I must have been around six—the birds flew directly at my head. So feeding the chickens was terrifying, and I wouldn't have missed it for the world. Besides, I'd already seen their earlier incarnation in the incubator, where row upon row of temperature-controlled warming drawers held fertile eggs about to hatch. I had stood there with Mamaw in the evenings, watching the shells crack and then move, finally seeing the wet, yellow cottonballs come poking out of their shells. The chicks were part of the long march that went from cute to kamikaze to Mamaw's Sunday fried-chicken platters, and I absorbed this inevitability as part of the farm's moral and economic quid pro quo: You took care of what you had— bean plants, fruit trees, chickens—for as long as seemed reasonable, and then you let them take care of you.

For years after my grandmother was gone, I believed she was tall, until my mother laughed at my memory and corrected me: Mamaw was only five foot four. But to me she was a tree of a woman, someone who moved patiently through the world with grace and force and never stopped, and I suppose this child's view was an accurate assessment. She had borne six children, five of them girls, and she had had to bury two of them before her death at eighty-three. My mother would worry over Mamaw when I was a teenager, saying, "No mother should ever have to bury her children," and I grew up sensing that this was the great divide, the one thing God shouldn't force upon you. Mamaw's only son, Jerome, named after Granddad, had been killed in a car accident when he was twenty-one, and she had gotten up from that and then seen two of her daughters struggle for years with depression. My grandfather blamed himself for Connie's and Ruth's sorrows—he came from a time and place where such troubles were seen as family curses, or legacies, and my mother told me once that he had said to Mamaw, with anguish, "It's my fault—it's on my side of the family."

Given what we now know about the genetic predisposition toward depression, there was doubtless some truth to what Granddad said, but not for the reasons he presumed. He viewed those handed-down torments as an act of God rather than biology, and his grievous sense of agency only made him mourn his daughters' troubles more. He had been raised as a Primitive Baptist, the evangelical wing of the Baptist Church, where his beautiful voice had led him to the a cappella glories of Sacred Harp singing, a musical outlet that had allowed a little celestial light under the door. But the Primitive Baptists had a dark worldview, much of it spawned from the Calvinist notion of election, and early-twentieth-century rural Texas was fertile ground for such assumptions—what God had wrought, man endured, hoping for redemption but never being so arrogant as to expect it. Granddad's sister, Georgia Jean, had died too young, and I remember stories about him shaking his head to Mamaw or my mother, saying, "Georgia Jean was just no good." This taint, he felt sure, explained the curse he had passed on to his daughters, and he carried that burden of belief throughout his life. Long after his death, I learned that Georgia Jean's depravity, as Granddad perceived it, was the dual affliction of alcoholism and depression. My discovery clarified his sense of shame and futility, for the moral and religious prognoses for these conditions were far more dire and condemning than a medical one would be a century later.

My grandmother was less beholden to such determinism. As the daughter of the severe Grandpa Mitchell, who made his kids stay on their knees in prayer for half of Christmas Day, she held to the word of God but not to the grimness of the Primitive Baptists, insisting that her children be raised within a sunnier realm, where free will had a fighting chance. She was a teacher before she was a farm wife, and most of her life was spent raising things until they could make it on their own, whether students or baby chicks or her own brood, and I believe this realism about her influence bought her some peace of mind in a world of hurt. When she booted my mother, Ruby, out the door at eighteen, she must have known her first daughter could handle the responsibility that such a move entailed. For the last few years of their adolescence, Mamaw had watched her two oldest girls take the bus each day into Breckenridge to high school, where they stayed past dark every night on the basketball court. My mother, four inches shorter than her sister Connie, was guard and captain of the Breckenridge girls' team, and in 1932, with Connie as star forward, they had gone all the way to states and won the championship. Connie was a tall, gangly woman with long arms and fingers, but my mother at her most upright was five foot three, and I was amazed when I learned she had herded her team to such a victory. But Mom, I said, to explain my surprise, you're so *little,* and she got a light in her eyes and said, "I know I am, honey, but I could really jump."

She jumped all the way to Abilene, seventy miles southwest of Breckenridge, and got a job as secretary to the county agent, typing cotton contracts for the government until she was as fast on her Underwood as a ragtime piano player. After two years of business college and enough cotton contracts to buy that 1937 Plymouth coupe, she headed for Amarillo in 1939. A metropolis compared to Abilene, Amarillo was way up in the northern part of the state, over three hundred miles from Breckenridge, and my mother went there at the end of the Depression, knowing the jobs were better and the sights higher. The deputy tax collector hired her to work in the front office, handling and typing the tax rolls for all the land in Potter County, and one day in 1941 a tall, dark-haired man came in and started raising hell about his excise tax bill. My mother was the recipient of this tirade, and so she stood a little straighter and her voice got quieter as he railed, and by the time she was through with him the man had stopped ranting and was trying to get her phone number. She wouldn't give it to him, but he got it from someplace else and started pestering her to go out with him, and thus began a courtship between my father and the one woman who had ever refused to buckle under his force.

This story, of course, became legend in my family for romance and chutzpah. My parents were twenty-seven when they met, an ancient age to be single by midcentury standards, and their footloose status suggested the independent streak each possessed.

During the early months of their romance, my father still had a redheaded girlfriend in Lubbock named Joyce with a jealous temper, and he brought up her name whenever he wanted to torment my mother, who maintained an exasperatingly calm veneer. Then one day he made a mistake. Out of town for a few days on business, he'd written letters to both women, and he put them in the wrong envelopes. When Joyce got the letter that began "My Darling Ruby," she went on a rampage and drove to Amarillo from Lubbock to confront the author. When my mother got the letter meant for the redhead, her composure served her brilliantly. She stonewalled my father, refusing to take his calls or speak to him, and her silence nearly brought him to his knees. By the end of the week, she had her boss answering the phone for her at work. He would tell my father that Ruby was unavailable, then hang up and shake his head at my mother, saying, "Poor Bill."

After that the game was pretty much set. He phoned her to propose from Sioux City, Iowa, in the spring of 1943, when he was on leave before shipping overseas. She rode a train from Texas for three days, and married him in a Baptist church with two elderly ladies off the street as witnesses. They had a two-dollar T-bone steak to look forward to that evening and the start of a two-week honeymoon. So began one of the millions of wartime marriages that would solder the next decade and define the social infrastructure of the next generation.

Because they had known each other for two years by the time they married, the epistolary relationship formed by my father's

years in England would not have been as make-or-break as those
of some World War II romances. But the portrait that emerges
from those letters is that of a couple on fire with love, sobered by
the enduring reality of the war, their sights set on a tomorrow that
was under siege. I asked my mother once, long after I was grown, if
she believed her generation had been happier than mine, and before the question was half out of my mouth she interrupted with
an emphatic yes. She responded just as swiftly when I asked her
why. "Because we didn't expect as much," she said, and while I
think this answered the question for her, it simply opened it up
for me.

In many ways they expected far more, if you measure their
hope by the distance between global catastrophe and the sweet
possibility of a backyard with a swing set and a couple of healthy
kids. It was a long march between the Third Reich's dream of
world domination and a ship docking in New York in 1946; and
the route became even more convoluted and trip-wired if you
gauged it by a soldier's pain or a young woman's fears at three
a.m. The men and women of my parents' generation may have
belonged to a pre-atomic age, but it is a fallacy of hindsight that
we ever perceive this as innocence. If they had yet to glimpse the
species' capability to self-annihilate, they already had plenty of
evidence that such a feat was possible. They contended instead
with the ordinary dangers of hunger, cholera, childbirth, a bullet
or a land mine on a field in France. They handled these threats,
looming or uncertain, with the same adaptive genius humans
have always used to face down fear: They counted on hope, they

fought their troubles head-on, they shod another horse or made a pie. In the case of my parents, they wrote long, intimate letters and counted on love.

Every American schoolchild has certain dates from the war inscribed in memory: June 6, 1944, when the Allied forces stormed the beaches at Normandy, or August 1945, when the mushroom clouds appeared over Hiroshima and Nagasaki. We tend to pay less historical attention to May 8, 1945, the day of the official German surrender, which became known as V-E, or Victory in Europe, Day. Roosevelt had died a month earlier, within days of the liberation of the camps at Belsen, Buchenwald, and Dachau. Upon the German surrender, Winston Churchill, declaring V-E Day a national holiday, was stormed in the streets of London by crowds of people weeping. In Amarillo, at the end of a workday, my mother wrote my father a two-page, single-spaced letter—one of the hundreds she sent to England, this one composed when she knew he was on a forty-eight-hour pass to London to celebrate.

Amarillo, Texas
May 8, 1945
Tuesday Afternoon

Bill, Darling,
   The first words of every radio commentator and head-line in any paper for the past twenty-four hours that I have

seen or heard has begun: "At 8:00 a.m. Tuesday Morning, (C.W.T.) May 8, 1945, the President of the United States, the Prime Minister of Great Britain, and the Premier of Soviet Russia will simultaneously proclaim the uncondi- tional surrender of Germany to the Western Allies & Rus- sia. . . ." [her ellipses] *It is here, Bill, the day we have all prayed and hoped and worked for so long, but you have mistaken the enthusiasm which would possibly have been displayed in Amarillo. There is nobody on the streets; the soldiers at Amarillo Field are restricted, I suppose; the liquor stores and beer bars are closed until Wednesday; the MPs are walking the streets; the churches have opened, and the stores closed for prayer and church services from 10:45 this morning till 1:00. Work is going on as usual in the business buildings and banks; there are no V-E Day Range Rider Victory platforms, either.*

I set the alarm for 7 a.m., and heard [war correspon- dent] Martin Agronsky tell of the stubbornness of the Ger- mans; if we have somebody like him talking every morning about how we shouldn't go soft for the Germans, maybe they won't soon forget the Allies mean business this time. I wasn't impressed by Harry Truman's proclamation (but gave him credit for first mentioning the fact that Franklin Roosevelt should have been here to share this joy); but when Winston Churchill came on (recorded to the U.S.), I stood there crying, with my slip on, one stocking down and one up, my hair tangled, and one shoe on and one off. You al-

*ways remember that, please, and keep this letter for our
children 25 years from now. . . . [her ellipses] in a little
3-room apartment at 516½ Harrison Street in Amarillo,
Texas—out here in the North Panhandle of the United
States of America, your wife, among probably 10 or 12 million other wives, stood with my hand over my heart when
they played the National Anthem—stood and thanked God
that with his help, our boys had won half of the battle, and
you were still safe.*

I HAVE A PHOTOGRAPH OF MY MOTHER taken sometime in the
early 1940s, leaning against a lamppost in Amarillo, a little
brunette with her head cocked toward the camera, her hands
clasped behind her back. She looks indomitable behind that
flirty, feminine pose, though perhaps I am only bestowing the
toughness and intrepid spirit that I knew all my life was there.
And yet no visual image could ever surpass the literary one she
gave me in that letter—a young woman standing at attention,
one stocking up and one down, weeping before the words of
Churchill and waiting for her love to come home.

Like an entire generation of midcentury Americans, my
mother found ways of navigating a world war, an economic depression, and a patriarchal culture that needed its women far
more than it compensated them. Most of her choices about
motherhood, marriage, and independence were made for her be-

fore she was old enough to walk. She did not disdain these paths but made them work to her advantage, much the way she had employed stony silence to bring my father to heel. Wildness was not an option for her—Georgia Jean had taken care of that—but feistiness was, and she stood as tall within those parameters as I believe any woman of her station would have dreamed. Her contentment with her life partly explains her shock when her younger daughter started protesting every cultural and social norm in sight. But she tried to understand the rough outlines of my tempests; she shielded me from my father's hurt and anger and, I believe, shielded him from mine.

These are the diplomacies common to motherhood; more striking to me now is what she left out of the instruction book. She had her children during the Eisenhower years and brought them up in a stronghold of religious and cultural conservatism, and yet I had no sense of being burdened with the yoke of preordained domestic bliss. In a world where Barbie reigned, I never owned one of the mutant princesses; I am told I didn't play with dolls of any kind. And I recall not a shred of a little girl's fantasy to walk down the aisle. I would never be a bridesmaid *or* a bride; history had rescued me from the pastel, dyed-to-match fate to which unluckier girls had to submit. My dreams about my future tended toward the less relational, and my most visual recollection belongs to my midteens, after I'd discovered the elegant world of numbers. I had an image of myself as a quiet, brilliant mathematician, wearing a white lab coat and big tortoiseshell glasses— I would carry chalk around in my pockets and scribble marvelously arcane equations on infinite blackboards. Tellingly, the room in this reverie is not crowded. An admiring colleague or two may have been in attendance, but there were no cheering crowds; certainly no one was throwing rice.

So this would be my fantasy in white: one about mastery and solitude, rather than off-the-rack choices or sidelined dreams. Can I thank my mother for such an open-ended plot, or was it a result of the novels I read, or maybe my own hardheaded personality? I know only that, on this front at least, she did not challenge me: never tried to marshal me into somebody else's master plan. Because my mother had grown up in a world where adversity was assumed but not sought, she knew, I think, that want and luck were only two components of a complex equation, and that there were no guarantees, God-given or otherwise. Despite the Baptist heritage—all that stern talk on either side about sin and election— she'd long since realized that what you got had little or nothing to do with what you deserved.

Chapter Eleven

To my aunt Connie I would owe my long arms, my swimmer's constitution, my weakness for dogs, novels, and bourbon. Also a propensity for introspection, what my mother would call brooding, that borderland poised, neutral as Switzerland, between thought and despair. The similarities between us, physical and emotional, were evoked throughout my adolescence; as with my uncle Roy, such comparisons could be made in wonder or dismay. She was a tall, lean, dark-haired woman, and of all my aunts on both sides of the family, she was my favorite. I alone of the cousins shouldered this affection, for Connie could be irascible and aloof at family affairs—only toward me and my father, I believe, did she display unequivocal warmth. She must have recognized us as members of that tribe for whom words mattered less than silent camaraderie.

During most trips to the farm, my sister and I were put in Connie's bedroom, at the front of the house, where we would lie under the cool late-night breezes of four windows and listen to the crickets and the cars passing on the farm-to-market road outside. It was here that Pam taught me how to crack my knuckles, here that we shared the last-minute confidences of sisters before sleep overtook us. We usually argued over who got to be next to the windows. I would lie there fighting to stay awake, looking out onto the milky Texas moon, smelling the night air of summer grasses and even the musky rock of the stone fence that ran alongside the house.

Connie had come back to the farm to live after her third marriage had failed. I was not old enough to remember her first two husbands, but the third was a sweet, kidlike fellow with strawberry-blond hair and rugged good looks. All the cousins liked Jaimie—he had a playful, roughhousing way about him, and he was a fireman, which impressed us all. He and Connie had met at the psychiatric hospital where they were both treated for depression. They found each other there like two soldiers wandering in from war, and their happiness and relief lasted for a couple of years, until Connie found out Jaimie was cheating on her, and then she filed for divorce and moved back home. Each day she drove into town for her job as secretary to an older attorney. Mr. Rice was wild about Connie and wanted her to marry him, though by then she'd had her fill of matrimonial bliss. Her life with Mamaw and Granddad was straightforward and simple. She gave them a little money each month, helped with the chores around the farm, and was left alone to do as she pleased—to read the piles of novels in her bedroom, or share a six-pack of beer with Granddad, or go fishing in one of the nearby lakes for largemouth bass or catfish. She had a spaniel named Duke she adored, and an old family photograph shows the two of them crouched by water's edge, at what must be the lake at Possum Kingdom. Gangly and brown, her jeans rolled up above her

knees, Connie is grinning, maybe laughing, with her arms out-
stretched toward her dog. She looks like the former star forward
of a champion basketball team, or a long-limbed Texas woman
who loves the water. She looks like somebody's favorite aunt.
What she does not look like, in this picture or any of the interior
shots of memory, is a woman on the other side of several hospi-
talizations and several sets of shock treatments. She does not look
like a woman who spent much of her life trying to outrun suffering, and who would die at fifty when she lost the race.

I WAS FIFTEEN WHEN CONNIE DIED, and I've always believed
modernity would have saved her. By that I mean that I loved her
enough to catapult her sad story a few decades ahead, imagining
that the treatments for depressed women who drank too much
would have progressed far enough by then to have given her a
fighting chance. Like Georgia Jean, Connie was born too soon—
wrong place, wrong time, as my father would say. She built her
little fortress out of novels and cigarettes and Duke's single-
minded devotion, and these resources kept her out of the hospital for years at a time and gave her some peace. But the Connie I
knew and loved was not encircled by a ring of sadness; I remember instead someone who seemed moody and mysterious,
which I interpreted as exotic. She had a rough, kind voice that
brought a calm to my young heart. She let me read her books.
She ran her fingers, long-nailed, through my hair and then left
me alone. She knew how to be with kids, or at least with me,

which was to make room in her own quiet zone and let me hang out there beside her.

Only once did I see Connie's equanimity shaken, when one summer afternoon I had done something to irritate her—my sister and I were being rowdy in the front parlor, I think, and I'd ignored Connie's first admonition to settle down. Having run out of patience, she thumped me on the head and spoke a few sharp words in my direction. I was crestfallen and stayed that way, long after she had forgiven me and tried to make up. I remember staring through the doorway into Connie's room, with its worn mauve carpet and low-slung vanity dresser, and being afraid I would never be welcome there again. For the rest of the day, even the air seemed dismal.

A child's memories are mostly sensate—we're not yet equipped with the vocabulary or analytic clout to make sense of what we see, and so we remember the cast of light, the smell or signifier that elicits yearning or fear or joy. My strongest memories of my aunt have a spatial distinction, as though her lanky, soft-spoken presence in my life would also define its emotional interiors. I had no direct experience of her troubles. But I knew these things the way children always know, by innuendo or atmospheric weight, through a kind of psychological osmosis. I knew, for instance, that Mamaw worried about her. I knew that the beer in Connie's hand was always cold, though I didn't yet know what that implied. More important to me then was the welcoming stillness of her spirit and even her room, whether she was in there or not.

This sanctity had been tested when I was eleven, when my mother found me immersed in the unexpurgated version of *Lady Chatterley's Lover*. I don't know that she had read Lawrence's novel, published in the United States, dirty parts intact, only two years earlier, but she knew enough of its licentious nature to want to keep it from her daughter. By the time she discovered me, though, I was halfway through the book, and I'd already found out about the gamekeeper and where he was putting those garlands of flowers. I was too young to think to hide the novel. My mother must have sensed this; I remember her saying, kindly, that I wasn't supposed to be reading it. Connie's rebuttal was swift but just as gentle. When she walked in and saw that I was taking the rap for her literary tastes, she argued my mother down on the spot. My mother usually assumed the older-sister role with Connie, but this once she submitted, and I have never known why. Was it the reasoned authority with which Connie spoke—she who knew books better than children, but who was so fond of me? Her self-assurance must have set the tone; I remember the tempo of her voice and my mother's prompt surrender. I suspect, too, that Ruby was half relieved by Connie's intervention. However protective in most arenas, my mother was intuitively libertarian when it came to reading; she would not have relished taking any book away from me.

After my brief affair with Lawrence, no one paid much attention to what I read in Connie's library. It was there that I first tried to read Faulkner ("The Bear"); there that I met the wondrous Atticus Finch of *To Kill a Mockingbird*. Years after Connie's death, my mother gave me her sister's old edition of the Harper Lee novel. Connie's carefully slanted signature is on the nameplate, and when I open it, I can smell the farm, with its cool front rooms and its mix of perfume and old furniture. My crumbling paperback of *Lady Chatterley's Lover* bears a more haunting and peculiar imprint of memory. I cannot be sure this copy was Connie's—I remember holding a bigger book there on her floor, but maybe that is because I myself would have been small. Still, this edition, printed in 1959, would be the right age. As with any well-worn book, it falls open to a particular page where readers have been before—in this instance, to the beginning of Chapter III, where the first sentence makes me start with recognition: "Connie was aware, however, of a growing restlessness."

So there she was, my dreamy, difficult aunt, cast as the star of an English tale of passion! Of course she was restless, stuck on the farm with Mamaw and Granddad—who wouldn't be? And yet here was another world, where a virile gamekeeper awaited her. I don't know how utterly I made this leap, though memory insists that I felt a frisson of delight when I encountered Connie's namesake, lolling about in Lawrence's parallel universe. I was still young enough to marvel at the half-mystical passage between fact and fiction, and old enough to understand the difference with fanciful regard. Connie's bedroom, with its library books and new hardbacks and airy country light, was a breezeway for me between the obligations of reality and the steeper climbs of the imagination. No wonder I liked to think of her as inhabiting both.

As with most emotional legacies, Connie's to me—her melancholy stillness, her little vault of print—would shift and lengthen over time, particularly in the years after her death. As I learned more about the difficulties she had faced, I began to wonder if I'd known her at all. Mine were only a child's shards of connection, a few moments of peaceful pleasure and affection, most of them sheathed in the half-light of Connie's front room. By the time I was old enough to consider my memories, though, Connie had already given me something more precious that I didn't recognize or articulate for years. Beginning somewhere in the gamboling innocence of childhood, then far beyond, the real Connie—*my* Connie, with her summer tan and her familiar sadness—became the visual referent for every tragedy I read. Connie's was the face I saw when I envisioned Anna Karenina, sick with guilt and passion and not knowing where to turn. She was the black-sheep brunette I met in so many stories of romantic doom, trapped on the rocks of fate. Over time she became Wharton's Lily Bart and every other woman who reached for the vial of laudanum—she was the wild, unhappy one, the woman whose dreams had died in the dust, mixed up with so much of America's sweat. Connie was all those women who had walked out into the wind. I knew her wind was private and scary and there were no other witnesses to its howl. And so I held her this way in my mind's eye for years: She was my fallen heroine on the High Plains, she was Tess on the Texas moors.

. . .

CONNIE'S DYING WAS A FLUKE, if indeed living in the road ruts doesn't lean you toward bad luck of all kinds. In her late forties, she developed aplastic anemia, a bone marrow disorder, as an idiosyncratic and toxic response to the hair dye she used and the medication she took for depression. With aplastic anemia, the bone marrow fails to produce blood cells, including platelets, which means its victims can bleed to death. Connie went downhill fast and died within a few weeks of being in the hospital. My mother was already with her in Breckenridge, so my father woke my sister and me early one morning to make the drive to the farm for Connie's funeral. I have almost no memory of the day: nothing from the church service or the graveyard, no scenes from the farm or with the extended Groves family. And yet two details are static and inviolable. I know there was no sun that day, that the gray, unchanging landscape of mesquite against the horizon was for me as bleached of color as a fifties newsreel. And I have a fragmented image of the dress I wore, a black linen sheath with a scalloped panel at the hem, which fell just below the knee. All I can see in this half-frame is the line of that hem, against the backdrop of the seat of my father's car. What my inert picture tells me is that I must have been staring downward for most of the long drive home.

ENDOWED WITH STRENGTH or holding bad cards from the outset, the women in my family did not suffer that economy of spirit that makes you poor in the end. The troubles I heard about or glimpsed firsthand—Mamaw's mourning of her daughters, the stories about Georgia Jean, my own concern for the aunt I loved— would forge how I felt about the anguish of others as I grew up. Compassion can be a foreign concept to an adolescent; certainly I lacked it when it came to strife within my own family. Rarely did I grasp my father's anger or my mother's fear, most of which were directed at me or my pursuits. But the secondhand sorrows, the ones murmured about or shared more as story than as crisis, gave me an undemanding chance to be sympathetic from afar. They taught me that you couldn't always get your car out of the ditch, no matter how tough or determined or self-starting you were. And they probably consoled me, reflecting as they did the black stars in my own emerging galaxy, a place of teenage despair and moody hormonal reach that I couldn't yet name but didn't exactly hate. I needed to know, I think, that you could be sad and half crazy and still have a life that meant something. I needed to figure out for my-self, which I would do over the next decade, that sometimes these definitions concealed or shrouded a brighter truth—that what looked like an off-road ditch might well be another, better path. The novels I loved were littered with fabulous women who had stumbled before the social order: women in London or old New York or English villages whose fire had outlasted their breath. When I was fifteen I had shown my mother two willfully bleak poems I had written, shoving them across the kitchen counter toward her with sullen longing. She read them with agonizing slowness, then laid them down and looked at me. "These are good, honey," she said haltingly. "But—they're so *sad*." Of course they were: With the thundercloud drama intrinsic to adolescence, I had embraced the sadness at life's core. I was feeling my way in the dark, like a child blundering across the trip-wired territory of blindman's bluff. And so I needed these other women's sorrows, both to render my tragic sense of self and to disable it. I needed for Anna Karenina to throw herself under that train, so that I would never have to.

ALL OF US DEFINE OURSELVES in relation or opposition to the archetypes we create from the world around us, whether known or imagined. For most of us it is a cache of images from several re-alities: the kind uncle who taught us chess or helped bury a blue jay gets cobbled together with Babe Ruth or someone out of Dickens. If Connie in the years beyond her death had become merged with the tragic characters I knew from fiction, another figure would emerge in my literary pantheon that had the same spitfire autonomy as Della McElroy, drenched in her petticoats and ready for bear. Because the women's movement had ex-panded my sights beyond theory or provincialism, I saw this woman, whatever awaited her, as a blend of courage and possibil-ity: She was Isabel Archer before Gilbert Osmond took her down, or Dorothea Brooke freed from the tyranny of Casaubon. She was Lily Briscoe, the young painter of *To the Lighthouse* whose independent spirit makes her a chalice of hope for Vir-ginia Woolf's vision. Lily may be a bit player before the inimitable grace of Mrs. Ramsay, but her generative calm means that, by the end of the novel, she is the one left standing.

Trapped at dinner in the company of the boorish Charles Tansley, Lily fiddles with the salt cellar, pretending to listen but in fact pondering the painting she has left in progress. It is a splendidly Woolfian moment, when the detritus of social conventions is a stand-in for grander matters, and that salt cellar, for Lily, will turn out to be a formidable tool. As her companion talks, Lily smiles and nods and solves a problem of composition—she will fix the painting, she realizes, by moving the tree to the middle. She places the salt cellar just so on the table to anchor her vision, while Tansley natters on and on. "Then her eye caught the salt cellar, which she had placed there to remind her, and she remembered that next morning she would move the tree further towards the middle, and her spirits rose so high at the thought of painting tomorrow that she laughed out loud at what Mr. Tansley was saying. Let him talk all night if he liked it."

I knew this woman. Every woman I knew would recognize her; we had all been her—hostage to the domineering cheer of Tansley, her smile automatic and her thoughts a couple of rooms away. By the time I met Lily Briscoe, I had already discovered one of bourgeois society's little secrets: that women in the company of Tansleys, of whom the world had produced far too many, might seem to be engaged, but their minds were roaming freely in the meadows of their own consciousness. If they were as fortunate as Lily, they got the tree instead of Tansley. One of the revelations of feminism in the 1970s was that women had been faking it in the bedroom, but the real treachery was going on in the dining room, where Lily and a million like her were pretending to listen. Ten years after that night, at the end of the novel, she remembers the evening as the critical turn in the road: "She had only escaped by the skin of her teeth though, she thought. She had been looking at the table-cloth, and it had flashed upon her that she would move the tree to the middle, and need never marry anybody, and she had felt an enormous exultation."

Freeing Lily from her own overriding despair, Woolf had sent her painter out into the world to survive her. That same unassailable spirit would reemerge a decade later in Eleanor Pargiter, the elderly firebrand of Woolf's *The Years*—"a fine old prophetess, a queer old bird, venerable and funny at one and the same time." This seems to me a commendable fate. Might I someday get to be this silver-washed eccentric, rolling my trousers and roaming Truro's marshes as I age?

THE PEOPLE WE LOVE BEST are always mysteries. Sometimes the truth resides in what we cannot see or do not know to look for—the songlines written on the land that hold the stories that precede us. A couple of years after I had left Texas, when it was too late to turn back and after I had survived in the East long enough to call it my home, I phoned my mother to say that, for the first time, I had made enough money as a writer to list it under "occupation" on my tax return. "My mother and I both wanted to be writers, you know," she said matter-of-factly. "I'm glad one of us finally did it."

In all the years I had blundered along in search of my own footing, she had never given me an inkling of this wish. Unburdened by the demands of history or anyone else's dreams, I had wandered toward and finally reached a world far outside the plains I loved and loathed. My mother had neither begrudged me this journey nor expected it, certain that I had to make my own way. But she packed my toolbox with her great wit and forbearance before I went, and she stashed there, for long safekeeping, her desire.

I had left Texas with the frightening conviction that I was abandoning an entire past, no longer bound by the old laws of obligation or by geographical parameters. But the past has no compass; I know this now as surely as I know that the land itself has a voice, capable of keening. Anyone who finds this a pathetic fallacy has never lain on a rock in high wind. It's hard listening, God in the vortex and all that, because the answers there usually have nothing to do with the questions posed. You have to walk out into it to learn anything, and there are safer ways than the routes all those pioneer women took, one-way flights to nowhere that left us only legend and broken-down dreams. You have to be able to bear the keening but, worse, the silence, which is even greater than the wind.

WE BUILD OUR STORIES, like houses on the high mesa, with whatever is at hand: the lace and flotsam of memory, the words flung out, the distances forged. If we have any sense of hope, we scavenge for more; we keep rewriting the prayers. In spring I hung a tattered Tibetan prayer flag on the back fence, to dress up my roses in summer and to defy the icy monochromes of February. Because I am a pantheist and cannot read the sutras written on each panel, a friend and I have declared we will reinterpret the prayers: We pray for dogs, for finer roses, for flat water on the river, for plumbing that works.

My mother, too, grew roses, fist-sized blooms that smelled like yesterday's promises and sugar and sun. They were wine red and pale yellow, and they floated in shallow bowls filled with water inside the house in summer. We had swamp coolers then in dry Amarillo in the fifties, glorified fans that forced air through a cool-water system, and the vents had long plastic ribbons that fluttered in the breeze as it blew through the dining room and cooled the bowls of roses. My mother's prayers were always private, but the feel of them wafted through the house like hope. Those ribbons on the swamp cooler, I suppose, were her prayer flags, too—her colorful background petition of joy. She must have prayed for cooler weather, a good life, good girls.

Try as I might, I know my roses will never be the ones my mother raised. Instead I have the memory of that harvest and their thorny little progeny, adorned in threadbare Buddhist garb under the pale New England sun. I can count on their indifference; they care far more for light and compost than for blessings. So I will be their nurse tree, as my mother was to me. I will clear the land and someday fall upon it, and the prayer that matters most will belong to time's cascade.

In the last weeks of his life, I walked into my father's room at the V.A. Hospital in Amarillo one morning to see a man standing at the end of the bed and wrapping his feet in a cotton blanket. The man was about my age and wearing blue jeans, and because of the care of his gesture, I assumed he was a nurse or an orderly. "His feet get cold," he told me, almost apologetically, and reached out to shake my hand. His name was Chris Ryerson, he had done two tours of duty in Vietnam, and he was dying from the effects of Agent Orange. "Don't worry about your dad," he said to me that morning, one of dozens of consolations he would provide in the next few days. "He'll be all right. We'll take care of him. The veterans out here all take care of each other."

My dad was eighty-nine, and his mind now belonged mostly to the outer banks. For the past several years he had suffered from Alzheimer's, though he was spared the particular cruelty of the disease that wreaks havoc on its victims' sense of well-being. Instead he had become serene and unabashedly tender: If the John Wayne hero had surrendered his bluster, he had retained the Caldwell wit and a sweetness that for too long had been masked by pride. Throughout his decline he had managed to live at home with my mother; now his heart was failing. A few years earlier, sitting in his leather chair with his eyes closed, he had told me how he planned to die. "I have congestive heart failure, honey," he said, with the sense of earned relief that belongs to the very aged. "I'm gonna die in my sleep."

When they brought him into the room he would share with Ryerson, his physical stature had collapsed into the frailty of the dying: The man who had stood six feet with a fighting weight of 175 was now all silver hair and bent bones, an old oak tree succumbing to wind and sun. He knew where he was only transiently, and he would ask the same questions—why he was in the hospital, if something had happened to his heart—again and again. Yet he had spoken to me by phone a few days earlier with a resonance and clarity he had not possessed in years—a momentary phenomenon I am told can happen near the end of life, a last brightening before the dark. I had asked whether he wanted me to come; I was on my way to the airport as we spoke. "For this little old thing?" he asked, in the deep, soft voice of the old days. "Hell, no. I'll tell you what I do want, though. I wish they'd give me a roommate who could play poker, so I could make some money while I'm here."

Ryerson laughed when I told him this story, and said he had learned over the years not to get in a card game with a man like my dad. "The World War Two vets are all liars," he said with straight-faced regard. "They taught me how to play liars' dice. I used to tell them, I might as well just send a check."

Within the portal of intimacy that death can present, I saw Ryerson do things for my father in the next few days that seemed as much acts of grace as they were of mercy. He saved him his milk from each meal, brought him soft drinks from the machine down the hall, gave him rolled-up washcloths to hold on to when he was distressed. If my father woke in the night and was afraid, Ryerson rubbed his back or read to him until he went back to sleep.

BECAUSE HE HAD BEEN IN AND OUT of V.A. hospitals for years, Ryerson was part of the fluid hospital culture of chronic-care veterans. He had suffered several soft-tissue cancers as a result of Agent Orange, as well as a number of strokes that affected his memory and mobility, though he could still walk with a cane. Now he had contracted multiple sclerosis, and he had been told he didn't have much time left. His short-term goal, he said, was to get home to his failing Labrador retriever, in neighboring New Mexico, with the hope he could care for him until the dog's death. Two of his six children had medical conditions believed to be Agent Orange–related; his youngest son was now serving in Iraq, even though Ryerson had begged him not to go.

He told me these stories without rancor or regret. As I sat on my father's bed, trying to get him to drink or take a little food, Ryerson and I would talk—about the Vietnam War, about losing your dad, about watching your son follow you into battle. He had gone to Vietnam in 1968, had been in combat in the Central Highlands and at Ben Het, and had killed a man for the first time on the day he turned nineteen. God's birthday present, he said, and shrugged, and shook his head. He kept two dog-eared paperbacks by his bedside: what looked to be a soft-porn novel, its cover illustration a pop-art buxom dame, and a collection of short stories by William Faulkner. I don't know which book he read to my dad when he woke in the night.

During those timeless few days in the hospital, I realized I was part of a scene as sweet in its redemptive irony as I was likely to find. That I, the stubborn daughter, was sitting between two old soldiers from different wars, watching one care for the other and counting on them both to help me through. My heart went out to Chris Ryerson as utterly as it had to all those boys I'd wept over thirty years earlier, when I had been lucky enough to hate the war but not its warriors. Now I was in the room with the aftereffects of that long-ago lost sorrow, and I was witnessing a tenderness no doubt born on the battlefield, where, as Ryerson had said, the vets had learned how to shelter one another.

My father's frailty frightened me, but it also touched some ancient place that had to do with honor and history, like watching an elephant fall and die. One morning a new doctor came by on rounds, hurried and distracted, and Bill gazed over at him and said to me, "Who's that bastard at the foot of the bed?" I half smiled at the doctor and then blurted out, absurdly, "My dad was captain of his wrestling team in college." The man looked startled but had the composure to smile back and nod, and after that he treated us all with more kindness. It was he who placed the call to my sister on the night my father died, hours after being moved to hospice. "These old World War Two vets," he said to her.

"Sometimes they hear the word *hospice,* and they just find a way to go."

Ryerson stayed in touch with me after my father's death, even as his speech became progressively impaired and he had to use a keyboard to communicate. He was out of the hospital for the time being. His boy had come home from Iraq on R & R, and they were going fishing. Three different units of the V.A. were trying to convince him to return to assisted care; only the Vietnam veterans' unit, he wrote, understood his need to outlive his dog.

For the last few years of his life, Bill had asked me repeatedly if I thought he would make it to heaven. I told him I was so sure of it that I expected him to save a place for me. He paused, the humor outlasting everything else, and said, "What makes you think I'm going to get there first?"

So he would have liked what Ryerson wrote me about him in the weeks after his death. "He was a good man," he wrote, "and from what I heard a good father. I am sure that when he reports to Sgt. St. Peter he will get a salute and a 'Pass On, Soldier.' "

WHEN I WAS YOUNG, my mother, in preparation for Easter morning, would spend the Saturday before the holiday dyeing Easter eggs for her girls. I remember the smell of hot apple-cider vinegar, which she used to set the food coloring for the eggs, and the startling, magical colors they turned, blues and purples and pale rose. My father would get up early and hide them all across the backyard: in the crooks and branches of trees, behind rocks, inside flowers. My sister and I would run to the porch and behold his splendor, the dry Texas landscape already bursting into spring, and for this day adorned with colors from a fairy tale. Then we would rush to gather them, crying out in delight with each discovery. If we were too small to reach the highest eggs, hidden in the trees, he would lift us up toward the branches; these were the finest quarry of all.

At the end of the hunt, exhausted, I would throw myself in my father's lap and beg him to hide them all again, and so we would soon start another round. What impresses me now is not the innocence of my request, but its radicalism, the commendable audacity that every child possesses. Until a certain age, we believe we can halt time and even shape it to our will—that we can re-create the experience of anticipation itself. My plea to my father was for the ultimate mulligan: Return me to the state of not knowing. Bend Einstein's warp curve like Silly Putty, get us back to the Garden, fire back at regret.

We can't, of course, which is part of the point; no real do-overs in life or death. You can't go back: to unboarded trains, to pristine battlefields before the dawn, to love that ended yesterday in Texas. Instead we have this stupid, lovely chaos, this burden and blessing called experience, the high beam of the past that is supposed to throw light on the future. Instead what you have, if you are lucky, is the next round: the silence at Shiloh, the grasses blowing at Little Bighorn, the oak tree on the father's grave. What we get is the lead weight of understanding, which we have the grace to call gravitas.

⁘

I KNOW NOW WHY the body is laid out: so that you can sit in the room with death and be able to bear its final word. The body is laid out so that you can lay your head on your father's chest and know that the tears you cry there, the warm salt stains on the cold body, will not go with him, though of course they will. It is the earthbound proof of words like *lamentation*, all music and grief, providing for a while what Pablo Neruda called the house of absence. So that you can know unwaveringly, which will help in the weeks to come, that he—the great good force who gave you life— is gone, gone, gone. So that finally, after so many years of upright defiance, you can fall on your knees before him.

⁘

IN THE LIFELONG MATCHING of wits that defined us, Wild Bill got the last word, which I know would have pleased him and to which I willingly deferred. The preacher who officiated over his funeral was a relatively young man who knew my parents but not me or my sister; she and I had been gone from Amarillo for thirty years. He spoke with the family in advance of the service, taking care to understand our wishes about the eulogy. My sister called to ask me if there was anything in particular I wanted the pastor to know about our father. "Tell him he always made us feel safe," I said, grabbing for the fundamental truth that emerges in the first days of parental loss, when the sentry in the corner has been retired.

Two days later, sitting in the front pew of the church where Pam and I had been confirmed, we listened to a kind, personable description of Bill Caldwell: the loving father and husband, the master sergeant and businessman who had served his country and his family. Then the minister took off. "He always made his daughters feel safe," he intoned, gathering force, "sheltering them even through the turbulent sixties." In the midst of one of life's most somber occasions, my sister and I broke rank from our tears, shot a sidelong glance at each other, and rolled our eyes.

Overwhelmingly Protestant, the churches in the Panhandle are its social and spiritual keystones. Often their congregants have known one another for generations: They attend Sunday school with their doctors and stockbrokers and car dealers; they know whose kids got into trouble and whose turned out all right; they have an idea who votes Democratic, generally a minority population. My family's Presbyterian church has a prayer chain so attentive and dependable that I've long believed its members enjoy an inside track. "Put so-and-so on the prayer chain," I used to tell my mother, feigning levity but dead serious. This sense of God's divine availability is widely held. One time Mom asked her minister if it was all right to pray for a specific outcome, or if such meddling might be construed as willful self-regard. "Heck, Ruby, you can ask God for a new Maytag if you want to," the preacher told her. "He just wants to hear from you."

In my occasional visits to my family's church over the years since I'd left Texas, I'd heard all sorts of profundities and homilies from the pulpit, and I'd come to love the place for the edifice of goodwill it provided, despite its difficulty in separating church and state. The candlelight services on Christmas Eve are so affecting that I once began weeping inappropriately during "Silent Night"; so much hope in the midst of all that emptiness just pushed me past the margins of acceptable Texas restraint. On the other hand, I'd also heard an assistant pastor in his holiday sermon implore God to watch over President Reagan and give him the celestial backing to carry the day. If Amarillo has its share of steadfast believers in the will of God, plenty of institutions beyond the church are ready to step up and share the message. I remember opening the daily paper one Christmas morning in the 1990s to see, above the fold, a color wire photo of the starlit sky over Gaza, with the caption "Jesus Born in Bethlehem."

So I was not surprised to hear our preacher going off-course a little in my father's eulogy, and I almost liked his embellishment for its utter fiction. Bill no more sheltered me from the storm of the 1960s than that prison tower sheltered Rapunzel, but he would have cherished the idea of getting credit for it, especially when, on this day of days, I couldn't argue back.

·　·　·

THE COUNTRY HAS BEEN OVERRUN in the past few years with the last wave of funerals of World War II veterans, gone home to die like great schools of fish upon the shores. So many are being laid to rest in the nation's cemeteries that their military honors have been streamlined to accommodate them. There is, in particular, a shortage of buglers. That mournful icon of a soldier's burial—the lone bugler playing taps at the grave—has now been replaced by a recording of the military bugle call, played on tape or CD.

But this rendition is good. It is heartachingly universal, its technology a metaphor for the huge numbers who now warrant the send-off, in the same way that a 33-rpm reflects the culture that produced it. The day they played taps for my father, two ancient veterans in dress uniform folded the flag in military fashion, handed it to my seated mother, and saluted her. The wind was blowing hard out of the northwest, and the sun was too powerful a blast of heat for late September, and the spray of pink roses on the casket moved under the force of the wind like sea foam on the waves, beaten beauty against a cloudless sky.

I had forgotten that drivers in Amarillo pull over when they see a funeral procession coming. As with so many local customs in the Panhandle, this one has its origins in both courtesy and space. There is plenty of land to pull over onto, not much traffic to disrupt, and no one is in much of a hurry. So it is a right and simple thing to do, to pay your respects to someone headed toward you in a hearse. The cemetery is out east of town, bordered by acres of ranch land to the south, and the drive there is on a straight line toward open country, with gravestones on one side and wheat fields on the other. The luminous morning we were on our way to bury my father, I looked out the window from the backseat of the limousine and saw this beautiful, anonymous gesture: what looked like a mile of Texas strangers, the wheat blowing behind them and their hats off, their cars stopped by the side of the road.

I FLEW HOME WEARING HIS DOG TAGS, sentimental but necessary, and I packed three bullets in my bag from an old revolver to remind me how tough he was and that he had given that to me. He used to be immeasurably proud of the boots he wore, usually full-quill ostrich Lucchese, and to display this vanity, he would leave one pant leg of his trousers half tucked into the boot, a sort of High Plains fashion clue that showed off the leather. When I ribbed him about it he would counter that you could tell how rich a man was by how he wore his boots: Both legs tucked in meant he had two cows and was protecting his pants legs while he sat on a milking stool between both animals. One leg translated into only one cow, and was thus a humbler statement.

As with most Texas lore that is exportable by the truckload, I assumed this absurdism was half lie and half legend; Bill always said he had heard it first from Grandpa Groves. Certainly I had been more demure about my own Luccheses, which were merely goat instead of ostrich. When I went through security at the Amarillo airport, I took off the boots, which have a steel shank, and because I was rushing to catch the plane, I hurriedly jammed one jean leg back inside the boot. A policeman who was surveying outgoing passengers gave me the once-over, and when I met his eyes I got a slow grin in response. "The way you've got those pants legs," he said, "I couldn't tell if you were buying cattle or selling 'em."

I hadn't heard the reference in a decade or more, and I doubt most people would have had any idea what it meant. I smiled back at the man and didn't break stride. "If you've got any money," I said, "then I'm selling."

AMARILLO THESE DAYS is as full of swagger as it ever was, lots of posturing and tough talk amid the religiosity and starkness of vision that define the place. The population hasn't changed much in forty years; it's one of those remote cities, poised in the midst of the country, that hang on to their families and replace the dying elders with new generations who grow up and stay put. In this way the town replenishes itself without resorting to import, and thus retains its tribal quality. People complain about the isolation, but they tend not to leave and they say they don't want to be anyplace else.

Out west of town, on the highway that heads past the stockyards on to Adrian and Wildorado, there are still signs reading SEVERE CROSSWINDS in the midst of all that emptiness. Off the interstate—the old Route 66 that takes you straight to California and thus is the chief reason anyone has ever stopped here—the main drags in town are a blend of chain and regional businesses: muffler shops, pancake houses, a local chicken shack with a sign outside that reads HONK HORN FOR FRIED CORN. Drive-by imperatives are big in Amarillo. Like the rest of the state, the city is a car-dependent culture, with drive-through banks and drive-through liquor stores and speed bumps even on quiet residential streets. There are more than three hundred churches in the area, roughly one for every five hundred inhabitants, and these houses of worship are not shy about competing for recruits. One Church of Christ on a busy intersection has a message board out front that changes its invitation weekly, though the general theme remains the same: C H - - C H. WHAT'S MISSING? U R !

Stanley Marsh's infamous Cadillac Ranch, bane and glory both when it was envisioned three decades ago, is still intact on the outskirts of the city, though they had to move the installation a few years back to make room for progress. The Caddies didn't go far, just a mile or two down the road, and they're still buried on that blank prairie, nose down, as if they've just veered off some highway to heaven. But my Amarillo, the site for all those lonely legends a girl invents and leaves behind, is a windswept portrait now of memory and change. The drive-in burger joint that I circled in a girlfriend's baby-blue Mustang, or where I sat close to Travis in the end zone, was turned into a Denny's years ago. The old Silver Grill, as romantic as a New York Automat with its swoon-inducing smells of halibut and prime rib, has been gone for decades. Most of the town's steak houses and boot shops belong now to franchises, and the parking lots are filled with SUVs without much mud on the bumpers. These alterations are trifling next to the land, its irrigation wells spread like some holy design among the crops, its brown and green and golden vistas attended by tumbleweeds and wind and not much else. The sky changes never and continually and holds in its capacity room for scourge as well as rapture. A blackening cast can pass over only minutes ahead of a flash flood or tornado, though most days, by rights, are calmer. Most days, the offering you get from a Panhandle sky is beauty barely outdone by desolation.

WHAT WE HAVE OF ANYONE is so slight: the timbre of a voice, the leftover stories, the smell of a hunting vest. And yet so much of life is about the empty spaces; I finally learned that much from all that land. The vacuum will always define its opposite: prayer in the void, or hope encased by despair, or the languor of a silent, precious day.

Here, for instance, I have left out the river at dusk in autumn, the hard taste of loneliness about which you can do nothing, the view from the far rise. I have left out the elegiac presence and great consolations of the dead, who are always with us and who become the mirroring pool into which we gaze. And I have left out the way loss changes one's tread upon the earth, as though gravity itself were affected. But these are the mysteries for which there is no story; they are the air that circles the breaths we take, and they shape our lives as surely as winter, war, God, or luck.

THE WEEK AFTER MY FATHER'S DEATH, when my mother and I had gone through his papers and I had found Roy's service records, she asked me to help her with Bill's guns—a rifle and a shotgun and an old pistol that we knew didn't work. For as long as I could remember, they had been stored in the back of an out-of-the-way closet. He had always been a careful hunter, so what we didn't expect was that his rifle, untouched for decades, would still be loaded. I called the only friend I knew in Cambridge who could both appreciate my circumstances and handle a gun, and he talked me through disarming it. The rifle was a bolt-action .22 Remington that Ruby had bought for my father one of their first Christmases together, in the 1940s.

"Make sure the safety is on," my friend told me. "Take it outside and point the muzzle halfway toward the ground. When you pull the bolt handle back toward you, the bullets will start to pop out of the chamber."

"I used to know how to do this," I said, and he hummed the old theme song from Chuck Connors's *The Rifleman,* to make me laugh and to steady my nerves.

It had been decades since I'd held a gun, so I was surprised by how solid and familiar it felt in my hands. Surprised, too, by the rush of concentration that overcame me, no doubt a blend of adrenaline and memory. The day was fearlessly bright, Indian summer, and I was wearing gym shorts and no shoes when I went out into the backyard, onto my mother's silky grass. I stood there with the wind blowing and my hair flying, opening the bolt of the

rifle and ejecting a dozen bullets onto the ground, and midaction
I realized how I must look—a barefoot woman in the yard with a
rifle in her arms—and I remembered where I was and thought,
Oh hell, it's Texas, no one would even care, and I could hear my father somewhere laughing. I rechecked the barrel and the chamber to make sure they were empty, put the stock against my
shoulder to see how it felt. Then I took the gun inside, where my
mother was waiting, and broke it down.

My first great thanks go to my editor, Kate Medina, and my agent, Lane Zachary, who have been unwaveringly loyal and smart since the book's inception. Thanks also to my editors at *The Boston Globe* for their generosity in granting me a leave of absence. Louise Erdrich, beloved friend, thank you for knowing how the story began and ended even before I did, and for reminding me about the necessity of doubt. I had two other readers who were extraordinarily helpful: My gratitude to Andrea Cohen, for her fine poet's ear and her equally resonant sense of humor, and to Shannon Woolley, for her rigorous appreciation of the territory I was trying to mine. My sister, Pamela Morrison, located the jacket photograph as well as a few lost memories. Dick Chasin, thank you for understanding the arc of the narrative, and for your enduring kindness.

At Random House, Robin Rolewicz continually used her skills and heart to make the book beautiful; thanks, too, to Holly Webber and Vincent La Scala for their impeccable line editing. Closer to home, I want to thank Avery Rimer, Rick Weissbourd, and Peter Wright; if everything worth doing takes a village, I need you guys in mine.

I must make two posthumous acknowledgments. The first is

to Caroline Knapp, a singular woman and friend whose death in 2002 left such a hole in my heart that I had to write this book to fill it. The second is to John Ferguson, a man of meticulous grace and mind who was my editor at the *Globe* for many years, and who died in 2004. I cannot imagine this book without the imprint that each of them left upon my life.

ABOUT THE AUTHOR

GAIL CALDWELL is chief book critic for *The Boston Globe,* where she has been a staff writer and critic since 1985. In 2001, she was awarded the Pulitzer Prize for Distinguished Criticism. She is also an avid rower and lives in Cambridge, Massachusetts.

ABOUT THE TYPE

This book was set in Bulmer, a typeface designed in the late eighteenth century by the London type-cutter William Martin. The typeface was created especially for the Shakespeare Press, directed by William Bulmer; hence, the font's name. Bulmer is considered to be a transitional typeface, containing characteristics of old-style and modern designs. It is recognized for its elegantly proportioned letters, with their long ascenders and descenders.